SPECIAL
Just the Ripe
MELONS
50¢

SWEET
CANTALOUPES
40¢
BUSHEL

LOUIS

Art Photo 3147 Marcy St., Omaha Nebr.

Omaha
Times Remembered
VOLUME II

Published by the

Omaha World-Herald
company

John Gottschalk, Chairman and President

Boys on Parade

Father Flanagan and his boys participate in the Ak-Sar-Ben Floral Parade on Izard Street between 17th and 18th Streets on Sept. 20, 1921. Flanagan had founded his home only four years earlier. Holy Family Catholic Church is on the left. *(Submitted by Girls and Boys Town Hall of History)*

The Omaha World-Herald marked the close of the twentieth century with our first volume of **Omaha, Times Remembered.** That remarkable book captured the lives of everyday people in the greater Omaha area.

This book continues that tradition by producing another "people's history" as recorded by the people themselves. *The Omaha World-Herald* asked its readers to share their photos to help us illustrate the routine, the commonplace, the ordinary – what it takes to build a city.

Omaha, Times Remembered, Volume II, widens the brush strokes of Omaha's ever-changing panorama. From nearly 6,000 submissions, we selected these 300 photos to represent the tens of thousands of men and women whose hard work, skills and dreams built Omaha into more than "a land above a stream."

The result is another striking view of that land, its people and their realized dreams. Enjoy!

John Gottschalk
Chairman and President
The Omaha World-Herald Company

ACKNOWLEDGEMENTS
Omaha, Times Remembered, Volume II

Project Staff

Kristine Gerber, Project Director
Jeffrey Spencer, Omaha Historian
Jeff Swisegood, Writer
Herb Probasco, Copy Editor
Traci Winget, Project Assistant
Monique Harris, Project Intern

Project Assistance

Bob Bailie
Jeff Butts
Rhonda Gray
Dave Griebel
Betsy Reece

Joe Sova
Kyle Steenson
Steve Stevenson
Chuck Wood

Omaha World-Herald Library

Book Production

Interstate Tele-Marketing Inc.
Jacob North
Omaha World-Herald Direct Marketing
Paula Presents!

And, most importantly,
to the hundreds of people who shared their photographs and memories.

Omaha, Times Remembered, Volume II was a labor of love. To all those who helped in any way, we express our appreciation. Special effort was made to ensure the accuracy of the information for each photograph. However, information written on the backs of photographs and dates recalled by contributors may not have been exact. For historical accuracy, we welcome corrected and additional information, which we will forward to the appropriate archives and museums. Please send changes to the Omaha World-Herald, Marketing Department, World-Herald Square, Omaha, Nebraska 68102.

Withnell Hotel

Withnell Hotel, 15th and Harney Streets, was built by John and Richard Withnell. The building initially served as offices for the military. In 1878, the year this photo was taken, it was converted into a hotel and managed by the Kitchen Bros. from 1878-1882.

(Submitted by Jeffrey Spencer)

The Blum Farm

Robert Blum (front) and his father, August (on the right), on the Blum farm in 1882. The farm, near what is now 108th and Q Streets, is now the location of Blumfield Elementary School. *(Submitted by Wendell Kronberg)*

Flodman's Jewelry

An 1882 view of Flodman's, a jewelry and sewing machine store at 16th and Davenport Streets. In 1912, Peter Flodman (man with the beard in the middle) was the Republican candidate for deputy Douglas County assessor. He died on July 14, the day of the election. *(Submitted by Janice Huston, great-granddaughter of Peter Flodman)*

Prospect Hill Cemetery

The Joseph Robins family plot at Prospect Hill Cemetery, 33rd and Parker Streets, in 1883. Started by Byron Reed, the graveyard (known as Cedar Hill at the time) had its first legal burial in 1857. It is the oldest active cemetery in Omaha.
(Submitted by Stuart Lynn)

Buffalo Bill Comes to Town

Buffalo Bill Cody's first Wild West Show comes to Omaha on May 19, 1883.
(Submitted by Omaha History Center)

Who Was First?

For years, there was a debate over whether the first white child born in Omaha was Margaret Ferry or William Nebraska Reeves. According to a 1979 Sun Newspapers article by H.W. Becker, William was the area's first white child as defined demographically. He was born Oct. 2, 1854, just south of what was then the city limit. The first white child born in Omaha as defined geographically was Margaret Ferry, on Dec. 16, 1854. She was born near the site of the present Durham Western Heritage Museum. She lived only a year. Pictured here in a charcoal drawing are Margaret's parents, James and Margaret Ferry. Descendants of the Ferry family include the Begley, Moriarty, Shanahan and Ortman families; all still reside in Omaha.
(Submitted by Chris Ortman)

The Whirling Dervish

John Taminosian emigrated to America in 1893 from Armenia. After a year of struggle, he landed the part of "the howling and whirling dervish" in the Barnum & Bailey Circus, traveling to 29 states in two years. He was invited to appear at the 1898 Trans-Mississippi International Exposition in Omaha. John decided to stay, finding work with Woodmen of the World Insurance, and met his wife, Ellen Anderson. He went on to sell Oriental rugs at 4912 Chicago St.
(Submitted by Florence Young, daughter of John and Ellen Taminosian)

Brewmaster Storz and Son

Master brewer Gottlieb Storz and his son, Arthur C. Storz, promote Omaha for the Commercial Club Market Tour in 1906.
(Submitted by Arthur C. Storz Jr.)

Guarding Omaha

Fred S. Knapp in uniform of the Omaha Guards, which he wore from 1890-1892. On Oct. 24, 1894, the Omaha Guards organization was mustered into the Second Regiment of the Nebraska National Guard.
(Submitted by Wade E. Knapp, a grandson of Fred)

On the Move

John Bekins (left, front in buggy), owner of Omaha Van & Storage Co., in a lot just north of the Bekins family home near 19th and Izard Streets in 1900. John passed the company on to his sons, Melvin and Paul, and the name was changed to Bekins Van & Storage. The family sold the firm in 1997. *(Submitted by Frederick M. Bekins, grandson of John)*

South Omaha Financial Block

At left is the original Livestock Exchange Building, as it stood at 34th and L Streets in 1900. At right is the Stock Yards National Bank. Also shown is the 70-room Drovers Hotel. *(Submitted by Jeffrey Spencer)*

Tax Collector and Much More

Fred Elsasser at home, 2814 S. 33rd St. He held many positions during his lifetime, including tax collector, sales manager for the Omaha Lighting Fixture Co. and manager at Standard Electric Co. He met his wife, Emma, in the early 1900s while trying to collect a tax payment from her. He also owned the Elsasser Screen Manufacturing Co. and worked with his family at the Elsasser Hotel.
(Submitted by Helene Elsasser, Fred's granddaughter)

The Baltaz Kramer Home

The family home of Baltaz Kramer, 1406 S. 17th St., in 1901. Elsie and Edwin Kramer and Vera Streitz are on the steps. On the porch are Mary Kramer Streitz, Baltaz Kramer, Ed Streitz, Bertha Miller Kramer, Alfred Kramer (baby in carriage), Clara Kramer, John Kramer and Clara's dog, Boosey. The house, built in 1872, is now at street level.
(Submitted by Dorothy Kramer, great-granddaughter of Baltaz)

Party on Ice

A skating party at Brownell Hall,
10th and Williams Streets, in 1902.
(Submitted by Mrs. Thomas Marshall)

Cooking with Class

Elisabeth Webster's Cooking School taught
classes at 20th and Harney Streets in
1902. The classes trained cooks and
domestic helpers for well-to-do families.
(Submitted by Jeffrey Spencer)

In Training

Charles Brown (far right) trains for the
Omaha Fire Department in 1904.
(Submitted by Darlene A. Jensen,
great-granddaughter of Charles Brown)

Water Wagon at the Ready

Fire Station No. 2, 211 S. 10th St., in 1904.
(Submitted by Darlene A. Jensen)

The New Central High School

The land where Central High School now stands, at 20th and Dodge Streets, held the territorial capitol building of Nebraska. After Nebraska became a state in 1867, the capital was moved to Lincoln. The territorial capitol was torn down and replaced by the Omaha High School. By 1899 it was decided to construct a larger high school. It was built in four sections around the old school (partially visible in this 1902 photo) and completed in 1909. It is known today as Central High School.
(Submitted by Jeffrey Spencer)

C.F. Hermanek Co.

The C.F. Hermanek Co., 1312 William St., shown in 1905, was a general store that sold a variety of goods, including food, hardware and gardening tools. Hermanek was an immigrant from Czechoslovakia.
(Submitted by Charles E. Hermanek, C.F.'s grandson)

Mercer Hotel Fire

The Mercer Hotel at 12th and Howard Streets caught fire during the evening of Jan. 28, 1905. The fire caused a half million dollars in property loss, but no injuries or loss of life occurred. The Mercers were the major property owners in what is now known as the Old Market. They continue to own property in the area today.
(Submitted by Jeffrey Spencer)

Building Brandeis

The Brandeis Store in 1905. It took one and a half years to complete. This photo looks southeast from 17th and Douglas Streets. The Omaha Building is in the background. *(Submitted by Jeffrey Spencer)*

At the Courthouse

Frances Dargaczewski (far background, right) inside the old Douglas County Courthouse, 17th and Farnam Streets. She worked as a clerk of the District Court in the early 1900s.

(Submitted by Tom Buras, Frances' nephew)

Lake Manawa Tragedy

The Lake Manawa pavilion in the early 1900s. On the Fourth of July 1906, tragedy struck here. While 50 people waited for a boat to go to shore, part of the flooring of the pavilion collapsed at 11 p.m. Six people drowned, including Bessie Hiland, pictured here a year earlier.
(Submitted by Arthur L. Young)

Golden Anniversary

At 20th and Leavenworth Streets, in 1906, the home and grounds are decorated for the golden wedding anniversary of residents Fred and Anna Wittig Krug. In 1859, Fred Krug started a brewery in Omaha on the site of the Vienna hotel near 10th and Farnam Streets. In the early 1910s he built a larger plant at 20th and Vinton Streets. Despite Prohibition, the brewery continued to operate supplying a vast demand of non-alcoholic drinks. He built Krug Theater and Krug Park, both no longer in existence.
(Submitted by Jeffrey Spencer)

The YMCA Expands

A view of the crowd gathered for cornerstone-laying ceremonies for Omaha's fourth YMCA, 17th and Harney Streets. The building went up in 1906 and was described in newspaper accounts as the "finest YMCA west of Chicago." The $319,000 terra cotta structure featured marble pillars, an expansive lobby, a gymnasium and the Omaha Y's first swimming pool.
(Submitted by George Kieser)

Entertainment Fit for a King

Madame LaBonché (shown at left) descends by her teeth from the Brandeis Store to 16th and Farnam Streets during the 1907 Ak-Sar-Ben Carnival. Ak-Sar-Ben street carnivals (one is shown at right) were held each year downtown until the mid-1950s. At each carnival, a portion of a street was renamed the "King's Highway," in honor of the king of Ak-Sar-Ben. *(Submitted by Jeffrey Spencer)*

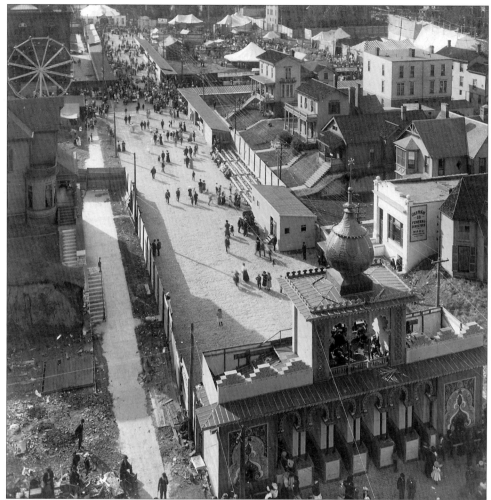

St. Cecilia Celebrates

On Sunday, Oct. 6, 1907, St. Cecilia Cathedral, 701 N. 40th St., celebrated the laying of the cornerstone at the church. The celebration included a parade of men two miles long and six abreast. The parade marched from 17th and Farnam Streets to 20th and Farnam. *(Submitted by St. Cecilias Cathedral)*

Trouble at the Schlitz

The Schlitz Hotel (16th and Harney Streets) burns on July 15, 1907.

(Submitted by John Sunderland)

Henshaw Hotel

The Henshaw Hotel, 1511 Farnam St., in 1910. Later it was known as the Diplomat Hotel and now is an apartment building.
(Submitted by Harold Rogers)

Old Market Entrepreneurs

Joe (left) and Tony Minardi at their vegetable stand at 16th and Howard Streets in 1908. They sold vegetables they had grown in their back yard. They later opened the T.J. Cafe, 503 S. 11th St. It is now the location of an Old Market tobacco store.
(Submitted by Kitty Schamber, Mary Brown and Kelly Dalhoff, great-granddaughters of Joe Minardi)

19

Already Landmarks in 1908

Aiming west from near 18th and Douglas Streets, a photographer in 1908 records a view of Mary Magdalene Catholic Church, Central High School, Air Dome Theatre and, at the far left, the Nebraska Telephone Co.
(Submitted by Wells Fargo Bank)

Transition on the Railroad

A retirement party for Union Pacific Railroad Vice President Adam Mohler about 1910. At far right is a model of the U.P. railroad headquarters, designed by W. R. McKeen of Union Pacific, that the company planned to build at 15th and Dodge Streets. The finished building, still standing, bears little resemblance to the model. McKeen also built the world's first internal combustion rail car in 1904.
(Submitted by George Kieser)

20

A Lasting Reminder

A traveling photographer captured Harry Rosholm on film shortly before he died in infancy. Harry is pictured in front of his family's home at 14th and N Streets in 1909. The home was a small three-bedroom house that included a kitchen and a parlor. There was an outhouse in the back yard, and the family brought water in from an outdoor pump. Their cow pasture is where Mount Vernon Gardens stands today on South 13th Street.

(Submitted by Frances R. Ahrenkiel, Harry's sister)

The Birth of UNO

On Sept. 14, 1909, 26 students gathered in the old Redick mansion (later renamed Redick Hall) at 24th and Pratt Streets to pursue their collegiate careers. Redick Hall is considered the first home of the University of Omaha.

(Submitted by the University of Nebraska at Omaha)

Trolley Man

Edward Gibson Hamilton (on step) was a conductor for the Omaha and Council Bluffs Street Railway Co. He ran the 30th and Spaulding line. This photo was taken in 1909. *(Submitted by Susan M. Thomas, great-granddaughter of Edward)*

Welcoming a Champion

A welcome-back ceremony for Frank John Riha is held in 1907 at Burlington Station on South 10th Street. Riha had won an international title in the V Slet gymnastics competition in Prague, Czechoslovakia. Riha, who became a Douglas County commissioner in 1933, died in 1966 at age 81. For 11 years he published "Naradni Pokrok." *(Submitted by John Riha, son of Frank Riha)*

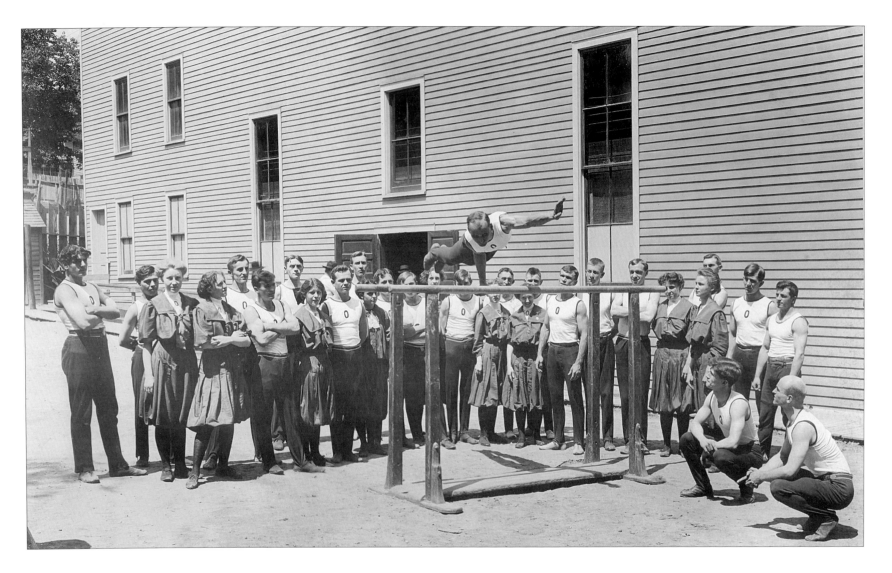

Parallel Performance

Frank John Riha balances on parallel bars at the Bohemian Sokol Hall, 13th and Martha Streets, in 1910. His brother, John R. Riha (far right) watches the performance. The hall, torn down in 1927, stood just north of the current Sokol Hall.

(Submitted by John Riha, son of Frank Riha)

Having a Blast

From left: Jenny Peterson, Mabel Hill, Olga Peterson, Edith Higginson and an unidentified friend at Hanscom Park in 1910. The group enjoyed riding the streetcar to Hanscom and picnicking in the park.
(Submitted by Alice E. Blackstone, daughter of Edith Higginson Hill)

Keeping the Streetcars Running

A line crew works on a streetcar around 1910. William D. Woodworth, (standing on rig just above its driver) was foreman of the crew and later general foreman of the line department.
(Submitted by Mrs. Byron E. "June" Palmer)

Holy Trinity Lutheran Church

Holy Trinity Lutheran Church, 90th and Harney Streets, in 1910. In 1901, Henry Bock, along with 10 other people, became charter members of the church. The church was dedicated in 1902. In 1920 the congregation merged with the new Immanuel Lutheran Church, 60th Street and Military Avenue.

(Submitted by Evelyn Bock, Henry's daughter)

Wartime Volunteers

Red Cross volunteers during World War I. From left, Bess Davis, Gladys Peters, Daphne Peters, Mrs. Coad, Mary Brinker, Mrs. Burns, Marion Towle Sibbernson, Dorothy Peters, Ethel Hamilton and Isabelle Johnston, wearing the goggles she wished she had taken off.

(Submitted by Mrs. Thomas Marshall, Isabelle's daughter)

The Galas Family

John and Victoria Galas were Polish immigrants who arrived in Omaha in 1911. They are pictured here in 1935 at their home, 4219 S. 38th St., with their 15 children. John was employed at Swift Packing Co. Front row, from left: Leona, John, Joann, Victoria and Dan. Middle row, from left: Edmund, Tom and Stan. Back row, from left: Wally, Mary, Edward, Leo, Annie, Joe, John, Ceal and Frank.

(Submitted by Kathryn A. Galas, Edmund's daughter)

Music by Laurene
Laurene Hulse Barnhart plays the piano at her home near 26th Street and Dewey Avenue in 1912.

(Submitted by Janet Barnhart Caulk, Laurene's daughter)

27

The Drew Family
Francisca, Clyde Jr. and Clyde Drew, Sr. pose with a cow in front of their home at 5006 Burt St. in 1912.
(Submitted by Jack Drew)

No Incorrect Clothing Here
Nebraska Clothing Co., 15th and Farnam Streets, opened in 1886 and was bought by John A. Swanson and William Holzman in 1912, the year this photo was taken. In 1929, John's future son-in-law, Otto Liljenstople assumed ownership. When Otto married, he took his wife's last name and became Otto Swanson. The firm, on a smaller scale, now operates in the Old Market.
(Submitted by Eva Swanson, great-niece of John A. Swanson)

Deadly Easter

A tornado cloud blows through northeast Omaha on March 23, 1913, Easter Sunday. The tornado killed 94 people, and 3,179 homes were destroyed or damaged. *(Submitted by Burnice Fiedler)*

Tornado Relief and the Day's News

The World-Herald set up a relief station after the March 1913 tornado. *(Submitted by Jeffrey Spencer)*

Surviving the Easter Tornado

During the Easter Sunday tornado of 1913, a pregnant Edith Waggoner Peterson went to the basement of her home with the rest of the family. Then she remembered having left a canary upstairs and went back for the cage, failing to get back before the tornado hit. The family piano was badly damaged, but Edith was unhurt. Her daughter Winifred was born two days later, March 25, 1913. *(Submitted by Sandra David Rockwood, daughter of Winifred, granddaughter of Edith)*

First Steel for the Fontenelle

The first load of steel for the million-dollar Fontenelle Hotel, 18th and Douglas Streets, is delivered by the American Transfer Co. in 1914. Omaha architect Thomas Kimball designed the 16-floor hotel in Gothic Revival style. He used red brick on the first 12 floors, and white terra-cotta above it, to symbolize the Indian and white heritage of Chief Logan Fontenelle, the son of an Omaha Indian girl and a French fur trader. The hotel opened in 1915. Its main floors were decorated in mahogany woodwork, velour panels, beamed ceilings and marble and tile floors. The hotel closed in 1971. *(Submitted by Harold Rogers)*

Laying the Groundwork

Alfonso Macchietto (second from left) and Severino Larese (kneeling) are shown after completing the terrazzo flooring in the old Douglas County courthouse at 17th and Farnam Streets in 1912. A year later, the two men formed the Nebraska Terrazzo and Mosaic Co. The firm later did work for the Joslyn Art Museum, the old St. Joseph Hospital, the Woodmen of the World building and Mutual of Omaha.
(Submitted by the Macchietto family)

Drive It with Flowers

An entry in the 1913 Ak-Sar-Ben Floral Parade. The leading automobile decorator was Estelle Fead, a baker accustomed to baking cakes. The Ak-Sar-Ben governors rode in the decorated cars. In the front seat are Mr. and Mrs. F.H. Davis. In the back seat, from left: Isabelle French Johnston, Helen Davis Roberts and Isabelle Eyland French
(Submitted by Mrs. Thomas Marshall, daughter of Isabelle)

Springing Into Fashion

The opening of the new spring fashions at the Brandeis Store, 16th and Douglas Streets, in 1914. *(Submitted by Burnice Fielder)*

High-Flying Fun

Art Smith was deemed "the most daring aviator in the world." He was known for flying as high as 5,000 feet upside down and built his own flying machines. In December 1914, he exhibited one of his machines and lectured on the science of aviation at the Brandeis Store. *(Submitted by Burnice Fiedler)*

A.C. Nanfito Groceries

A.C. (Antonio Cirino) Nanfito grocery store, 13th and Pierce Streets, in 1915. From left, on the wagon, Concetta Circo, Antonio Nanfito (holding his son Jake) and Alfio Scolla.
(Submitted by Meg Nanfito Jones, niece of Jake)

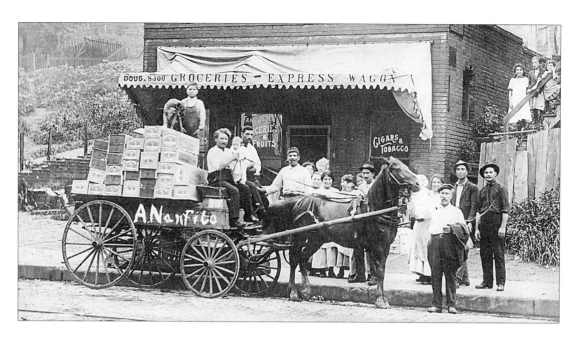

Ready to Tour

In 1915, Charles G. Hennings bought this Ford Model T Touring Car for $463.10. The price included gas and tax. Hennings went on to work for the Andrew Murphy and Son Chrysler dealership, located where Gene Leahy Mall now stands.
(Submitted by Steven W. Leypoldt, Charles' grandson)

The Milk Wagon

Magnus Christensen (on truck) delivered milk from the Christensen Dairy to north Omaha and South Omaha. The Christensen family owned two delivery wagons in 1915.
(Submitted by Richard Christensen, son of Magnus)

Life Before West Omaha

From left, Pauline Stolley, Fred Stolley, Walter Stolley, John Stolley, Peter Stolley and Florence Stolley at their farm near 156th Street and West Dodge Road in 1915. In 1960, the farm was eliminated and new homes were built in the area.
(Submitted by Marjorie Vaculik, granddaughter of John Stolley)

1916 Champions

The Murphy Did It baseball team, city champions in 1916. Art Moran (back row, center holding pennant) and Edward J. Quinn (front row, third from left) were players.
(Submitted by the Bain family)

The General Manager and His Team

The 1929 members of the Murphy Did It baseball team, sponsored by Bert Murphy, owner of Murphy Chrysler-Plymouth. The general manager of the team, Edward J. Quinn (top left) played for the team in the years before World War I.
(Submitted by John G. Quinn, son of Edward J. Quinn)

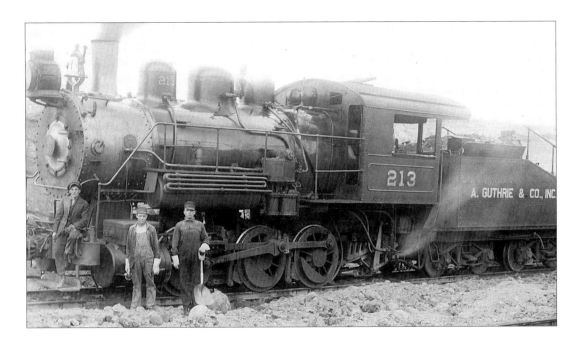

Keeping the Fires Burning

Tom Stoysich (holding shovel) was a fireman on this train in 1916. *(Submitted by Rudy and Rita Stoysich, Tom's son and daughter-in-law)*

Red Cross Occupies First Presbyterian

During World War I, all three floors of the new parish house at First Presbyterian Church, 34th and Farnam Streets, were in use as a Red Cross auxiliary. More than 600 women of the congregation provided linen, including pajamas, bathrobes and sheets, for the Nebraska Base Hospital in France. Jessie Millard, daughter of Sen. J.H. Millard, was in charge of the volunteers. *(Submitted by Mary L. McLendon)*

Sisters and Their Dolls

Surrounded by their dolls, from left, Mary Alice, Sally and Georgette Johnston play on the back steps of their home at 105 S. 49th St. during the summer of 1917.
(Submitted by Mrs. Thomas Marshall, in center)

A Ford Pioneer

From 1913 to 1927, W.P. Adkins (left) owned the Adkins Motor Co., South Omaha's first Ford dealership, at 24th and N Streets. In 1927, the Universal Motor Co. acquired the Adkins dealership.
(Submitted by Marian V. McKay, granddaughter of W.P.)

An Influential Teacher

May Scotland (front row 10th from left in bow tie), was dean of women at Brownell Hall, a boarding and day school, when this photo was taken in 1917. The building originally was the J. N. H. Patrick home and later became the clubhouse of Happy Hollow Country Club before it was converted into Brownell Hall. Besides being a teacher, May was a violinist. She graduated from the Institute of Musical Art of New York and also studied in Leipzig, Germany. Under her direction, an orchestra and glee club were begun at the school.

(Submitted by Conrad Young, May's son)

Mother's Little Soldiers

From left, Francisca, Howard, Clyde Jr., Jack and Louis Drew at their home, 310 S. 53rd St., during World War I. The Drews bought nearly four acres of land for the home in August 1914 for $20,000. The area was known as Drew's Dundee Acres.

(Submitted by Gary Drew, Howard's son).

Leo and His Sisters

From left, Bernadette, Leo Jr., Mary Jeanette, and Veronica Hoffman at their home, 425 N. 38th St., in 1918.
(Submitted by Pat Heese, Leo's daughter)

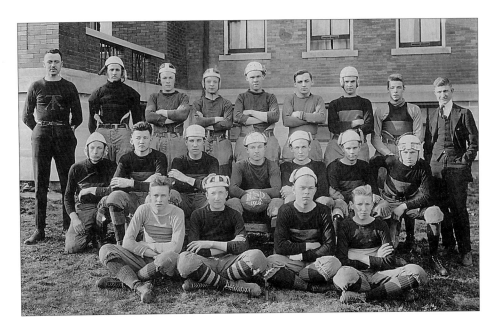

Hand Signals were Critical

Raymond D. Anderson (front row, second from left) played football at the Nebraska School for the Deaf, near 45th Street and Bedford Avenue, in 1918. The students resided at the school, and sports became a big part of their lives. A flashing light or waving arms were the signals to let the boys know when it was time to stop a play. In their huddles, players would sign the next plays. The Nebraska School for the Deaf closed in May 1998.
(Submitted by Lola Anderson, daughter of Raymond Anderson, and the Ray Anderson family)

Off to War

As a faithful employee of the John J. Ostronic Plumbing Co., Frank Hudece, standing, was given $5 and wishes for a safe return before going into the Army in 1918, during World War I. Frank became the first of three generations to serve in the Army. Frank's son, Robert, served in World War II, and Robert's son, Edward, served in Vietnam from 1970-71.
(Submitted by Lynne Richt, Frank's granddaughter)

Off to the Movies

Boys from Father Flanagan's Boys Home and other children are guests of The Daily News in 1919 to see the movie "Anne of Green Gables" at the downtown Sun Theatre.
(Submitted by Girls and Boys Town Hall of History)

A Patriot Visits

Irish patriot Eamon de Valera (with flowers) is welcomed to Omaha by John Rush (left of de Valera) in 1919, shortly after de Valera's escape from a British prison. De Valera was a leader of the anti-British Easter Rebellion and traveled as a stowaway to the United States to raise money for the cause of Irish independence. He raised six million dollars and later become president of the Irish Free State.

(Submitted by Chris Ortman, grandson of John Rush)

Swedish Mission Nurses

Gertrude Gatz Hughes (far right) and her nursing friends in front of the Swedish Mission Hospital, 24th and Pratt Streets, in 1920. *(Submitted by Mary Suzanne Hughes, daughter of Gertrude Gatz Hughes)*

Surgeon to the Rescue

Breaking ground in 1919 on the Medical Arts Building, 17th and Dodge Streets, initially begun with pledges. When the doctors failed to fulfill their pledges, the project went broke and construction was ceased. A prominent surgeon, E. Willard Powell (with shovel), who worked at the Swedish Mission Hospital, 24th and Pratt Streets, provided the money to finish the project. It was completed in 1926, two years before his death. The building was razed in April 1999 to make way for the 40-story First National Center. The ornate building in the background is the old Omaha Post Office, razed in the late 1960s to allow the building of a new First National Bank office tower and what is now the Doubletree Hotel. *(Submitted by Lucy Ann Powell Bean, daughter of E. Willard Powell)*

Making Forest History

Dr. Harold Gifford Sr. signs the deed conveying property that became the initial land parcel of Fontenelle Forest on Jan. 27, 1920. The deed was signed in the Omaha National Bank office of Sen. Joseph Millard. Those present are (from left): Sen. Millard, Mrs. William F. Baxter, William Stull, Frederick J. Adams, C.J. Ernst, Thomas R. Kimball, Mayor Edward Smith, Dr. Gifford and Roy N. Towl.

(Submitted by Gary Garabrandt)

The Brewers Knew Leo

Trained as a plumber in Vienna, Leo Baroch (pictured in about 1920) came to Omaha in 1887. He established this plumbing business at 505 S. 13th St. in 1888. In addition to providing plumbing supplies, Leo was the exclusive distributor for the Cleveland Pump and Faucet Co. He supplied Omaha saloons and breweries with a variety of beer pumps and was well-known to early Omaha brewers, including Gottlieb Storz and the Metz brothers.
(Submitted by David Krecek, grandson of Leo)

Bancroft Elementary Graduation

Bancroft Elementary School students celebrate their graduation from eighth grade in 1920. Among those pictured is Mabel Bahnke (center, hair pulled back). She graduated from Technical High School in 1924 and went on to become the head clerk at the Office of the Clerk, Douglas County District Court. She retired in 1971.
(Submitted by Phyllis Sorensen, niece of Mabel)

Final Exam

Mt. Saint Mary's High Seminary, a private girls school at 1424 Castelar St., was operated by the Sisters of Mercy. At the 1920 graduation dinner, girls were tested on their manners and proper use of utensils while eating their chicken dinner. A college was added the year Florence Shaw graduated from high school. The school became Mercy High School and College of Saint Mary.
(Submitted by Catherine Lynn, daughter of Florence Shaw Van Scoy)

Filling Up at the Manhattan

The Manhattan Auto Filling Station, 17th and Howard Streets, in the early 1920s.
(Submitted by Burnice Fiedler)

Leaders of the Prettiest Mile

Nina Adwers (far right) was a member of the original board of directors (shown here in 1920) for the "Prettiest Mile Club," a social organization in north Omaha. It later became the Birchwood Club. The group played golf at nearby Miller Park.
(Submitted by Bob Adwers, son of Nina)

Helping to Build Nebraska

Founded in 1883, Sunderland Brothers Co. produced coal, coke and lime until the turn of the century, when it expanded into building materials and marble. The company's marble can be seen in St. Cecilia Cathedral and the Nebraska State Capitol. The fourth generation of Sunderlands operates the company today. The company, now at 9700 J St., focuses on wholesale distribution of tile, kitchen cabinets and finishing products for commercial and residential use.
(Submitted by John Sunderland)

Yechout Paint and Wallpaper

Rudolph Yechout (left) at Yechout Paint and Wallpaper, 4725 S. 24th St., Sept. 18, 1937. Prior to starting the store in the 1920s, Rudolph worked at Beard Paint Co, 1209 Harney St. Rudolph ran the business until 1966. His granddaughter, Mildred Libota, worked as a bookkeeper for the business. In 1944, Mildred and her husband, John, became partners with Rudolph.
(Submitted by Donald Yechout, grandson of Rudolph)

Tuning In His Jell-O Radio

Frank Matthews plays with his first radio in the back yard at his home, 3502 Webster St., in the 1920s. Most homemade radios of that time were made out of cigar boxes, but Frank's radio had been constructed out of a Jell-O box by his father, Francis. Frank picked up music from as far away as New York.
(Submitted by Kathleen Matthews Irvine, sister of Frank)

47

Road Racers and Their Scrambola

The South Omaha American Legion's annual road race drew big crowds in the 1920s. Pictured here is a 1911 Scrambola, which was driven in the race by Joe Haney, seated in front and wearing a bow tie. Next to Haney is Johnny Krajicek, leaning on the steering wheel. Also pictured are Dr. Joe Yechout (far right) and, to the left of Yechout, Charles Hickey and Emil Stahmer. The car is parked in front of Basil Stella's service garage at 56th and Center Streets.

(Submitted by Donald and Rosemary Yechout, Joe's son and daughter-in-law)

Pure Refreshment

Everett Kemper enjoys a drink of fresh, cold spring water at Elmwood Park in 1938. During the 1920s, people would carry buckets to the park and fill them with spring water to take home. The spring was opened in 1910. It was closed many years later, due to water contamination. It was reopened in 2000 as the Elmwood Park Spring Grotto, but the water remained off-limits for drinking after tests revealed it was contaminated.
(Submitted by Allis Kemper, Everett's wife)

Chief Donahue and His Men

John P. Donahue Sr. (far left) was the second district battalion chief of the Omaha Fire Department, station No. 18, at 37th and P Streets during the 1920s. He worked for the department for about 20 years.
(Submitted by John P. Donahue, son of John Sr.)

From Ireland to Omaha

Ed J. McKeon (center) immigrated to the United States from Ireland in 1910. He served in World War I and started his own business, Central Dairy, Fifth Avenue and J Streets, in east Omaha around 1920. He delivered between 16th and 20th Streets, from Capitol Avenue to Locust Streets in the 1920s. The business closed in 1950. *(Submitted by John P. Donahue, nephew of Ed J. McKeon)*

Alexander's Barbershop

In the 1920s, Alexander "Teddy Bear" Simmons (second from left) opened the first black-owned barbershop in Omaha at 14th and Dodge Streets, where The World-Herald now stands. His son, Albin (seventh from left), who was 16 at the time, shined shoes and kept the barbershop clean. *(Submitted by Leella Payne, granddaughter of Alexander)*

When Downtown Was Bustling

Downtown Omaha, 16th and Farnam Streets, in midafternoon in 1921.

(Submitted by Wells Fargo Bank)

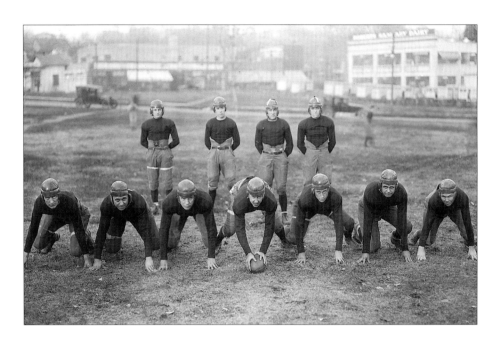

Tech High Takes the Field

The first football squad of the new Technical High School, 3215 Cuming St., 1922. Back row, from left: Richard Singles, Don Munroe and Harry Weisenberg. Front row, from left: Martin Swanson, Marcus Krasne, William Francis, Russel Pierce, Elmer Holm, John Doarn and Nelson Short.
(Submitted by Rose Baker)

Little Drummer Boys

The Field Club Grade School drummers, 36th and Center Streets, in 1924. Among the performers are brothers Jake Nanfito, front row-left and Charlie Nanfito, second row-left.
(Submitted by Meg Nanfito Jones, Charlie's daughter)

Lining Up With the Babe

The W.O.W. Insurance Co. baseball team with Babe Ruth at League Park, 15th and Vinton Streets (later renamed Rourke Park after a well-known local player), in the spring of 1922. Fifth from left is Bill "Banty" McKeague. In the dugout were Bill's nephews, Bud and Lou Dutch. The ballpark was built in 1911 and burned down on Aug. 14, 1936.
(Submitted by Margaret L. Dutch, widow of Bud)

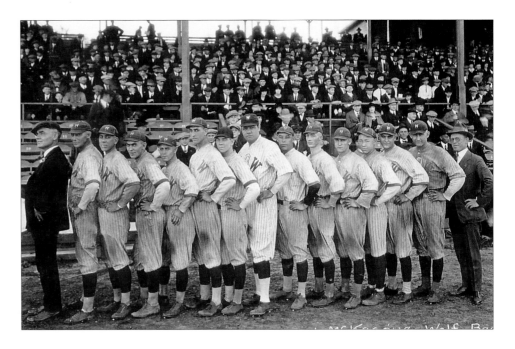

All Hail the Queen

Ruth Vest was crowned Queen of May at Bemis Park in 1923. Also pictured are heralders Lydia Ross and Carol Chaloud, jester Byran Clark (in clown robe), maids Marie Judson and Lillian Freeman, crown-bearer Eleanor Sherrill and train-bearer Rose Stein.
(Submitted by Omaha Technical High School Memorabilia Room)

Barnhart and Bryan

John W. Barnhart (far right) and William Jennings Bryan (fifth from right) attend a political dinner on Jan. 6, 1923.
(Submitted by Janet Barnhart Caulk)

Ladies of the Club

Eugenie Whitmore (center) hosts the Amateur Musical Club at her home Aug. 16, 1923. Participants include May Scotland Young (back row, third from left) and to the right of Whitmore, Mrs Harry O. Steele, Mrs. A.W. Gordon and Mrs. Harry Nicholson. Mrs. J.A.C. Kennedy is second from left in the front row.
(Submitted by Conrad Young, May's son)

A Famous Ford

The 10 millionth Ford came through Omaha in 1924. Driving the car is William Sample. Jack Hart, left, and Byron Hart, right, also pose with the car. Sample Hart was the first Ford dealer in Omaha.
(Submitted by Bob Adwers)

In Service for 70 Years

A 1927 view of the Nebraska Power Co. service building at 43rd and Leavenworth Streets. The building was then three years old. OPPD, successor to Nebraska Power, sold the building in 1998 to the University of Nebraska Medical Center.
(Submitted by Omaha Public Power District)

Budding Mechanic

From left, John Griswold, a neighbor boy and Clarke Griswold prepare to race in front of the Griswold home, 4419 Commercial Ave., in 1925. John had an early love for cars and went on to become an auto mechanic who ran his own service station in the Omaha area for 60 years - at 16th and California, 42nd and Leavenworth, and 55th and Military. *(Submitted by Patti Ybarra, daughter of John)*

Jobber's Canyon

Along the Missouri River front, east of the retail district, were the wholesale markets of Omaha. This was how the area looked in 1927. Known as Jobber's Canyon, these structures were torn down in the early 1980s and replaced by the ConAgra headquarters. *(Submitted by William R. Fead)*

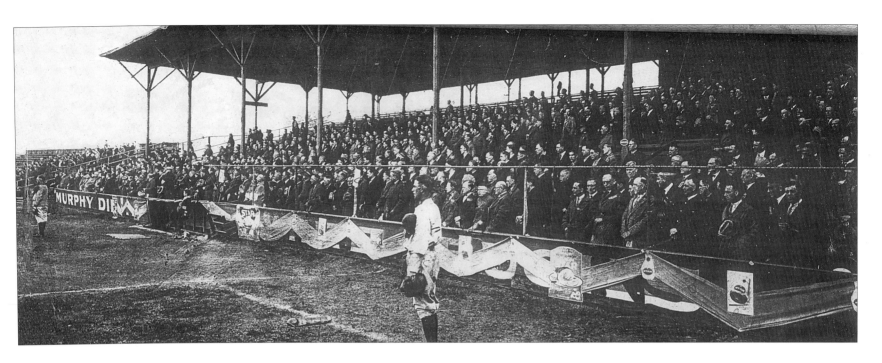

Omaha Baseball Park

City leagues played at the Omaha Baseball Park, 25th and Arbor Streets. This picture was taken shortly before the park was destroyed by fire in 1926. *(Submitted by Louie Marcuzzo)*

Christmas Glee

From left, Kenneth Golden, Walter Cady and Ezra McIntosh were members of the Senior Glee Club at Technical High School during the 1926-27 school year. The boys sang and helped sell Christmas seals for the American Lung Associaton. *(Submitted by Rose Baker)*

The Latest Best-Seller?

In 1926, 3-year-old Patricia Jane McDermott Dagleish practices reading on the porch of her home at 3328 Fowler Ave. Patricia went on to join the Navy during World War II. She was a control tower operator in Santa Ana, Calif., and also volunteered at Immanuel Hospital during the war. *(Submitted by Paul McDermott, her brother)*

One Last Parade

Ann Christiansen adjusts Scott Andersen's breeches for the Easter Parade while the 1776 lady, Lisa Hannam, stands by. Christiansen staged her 35th and last Easter Parade in 1976. Through various stages of rehearsal for the event that year, all but one of her Corrigan Elementary School students were stricken by the chicken pox. Christiansen taught in the Omaha Public Schools for 50 years, 46 of them at Corrigan Elementary School, 3631 Monroe St. *(Submitted by Ann Christiansen)*

A Taste of Home at Work

Rocho's Box Lunch started in 1922 when Walter Rowley, a structural steel worker, could not descend from his job on tall buildings in time to eat lunch and get back to work. So he asked his mother-in-law, Ellen Rocho, to pack a sack lunch. Then all the workers wanted one. The lunches were delivered throughout Omaha, and over 1,500 lunches were delivered to Union Pacific alone. The business ended in 1947. Employees pictured at Elmwood Park in 1926 are (from left): Grace Esbeck, Ellen Rocho, Gladys Rocho Turnquist, Stanley Redwelski, Billy Holmes, Gilbert Belland, Louis, Sam Lafreniere, Otto Lush and John Pullen.

(Submitted by Marjorie R. Towey, Ellen's granddaughter)

The Riviera in Its Heyday

After $1,500,000 worth of construction, the Riviera theater opened in 1927 at 20th and Farnam Streets. It was a member of the Publix chain and was recognized as one of the most beautiful theaters in America. Later, it was renamed the Astro. Today it is the Rose Blumkin Performing Arts Center.

(Submitted by William R. Fead)

When Omaha Buttered the Nation

In 1927 when this photo was taken off a creamery company dock near Ninth and Douglas Streets, Omaha led all other cities in the manufacture of butter. Products from Fairmont Creamery Co., Jerpe Commission Co., Kirschbraun & Son, David Cole Creamery Co., Roberts Sanitary Dairy, Harding Cream Co., Omaha Cold Storage Co. and Alamito Dairy were valued at more than $25,500,000. Omaha butter was served from San Francisco to New York and in London, Paris and other European cities. *(Submitted by William R. Fead)*

One at a Time
A group of children play at Hanscom Park, near 32nd Street and Woolworth Avenue, in 1927.
(Submitted by William R. Fead)

Decades of Lead

In 1927, when this photo was taken, this American Smelting and Refinery Co. (Asarco) plant at Fifth and Douglas Streets was the largest pig lead refinery in the nation. It was responsible for about 30 percent of the country's lead production. The company also produced gold, silver and bismuth. The plant was established April 4, 1899, and closed in July 1997. In recent years, the company was successfully sued for polluting the Missouri River. Controversy has swirled over the extent of soil pollution at the site, which is being capped as part of its development as an Omaha park.
(Submitted by William R. Fead)

Still in Business

Started in 1888, Brewer's Funeral Home (shown here in 1929 at 4609 S. 24th St.) was located at various south Omaha locations until 1990, when Brewer-Korisko Mortuary moved to its current location at 5108 F St. The clock in the picture was maintained by Western Union and was automatically monitored every hour on the hour. People would set their watches by the clock.
(Submitted by Jerry Korisko, partial owner and consultant and son of Jerome Korisko, an owner with his brother Walter of the business in the 1930s and 40s)

Ready to Tour

Margaret Shotwell, an Omaha socialite and pianist, sits for a picture before her American concert tour with Benjamino Gigli, a famous Metropolitan Opera tenor, in 1928. *(Submitted by Jack Drew)*

Robert's Dairy Fleet Team

Robert's Dairy Co., 2901 Cuming St., in 1928. From left: Ben Zahm, James Kearney, Earl Blackburn, Aage Petersen and Burney Combs. Ben was recruited to work for Robert's from Ford Motor Co. As a garage manager, Ben set up a fleet of trucks and assisted in the transition from horse and buggy to truck delivery. He retired from the dairy in 1965 as the general fleet manager and safety driver.
(Submitted by Dick Zahm, son of Ben)

South Omaha Cobbler

Alex Papp at Papp's Shoe Store,
38th and Q Streets, in 1929.
(Submitted by Rudy and Rita Stoysich)

Shoes by Holubar

In 1905, Joseph and Francis Holubar immigrated to
the United States from Czechoslovakia. Joseph Holubar
Sr. (left) and his son, Joseph Jr., appear in this April
1929 photo. The family-owned Holubar Shoe Store
opened at 5210 S. 21st St. in 1921 within the thriving
Czech business community in the Brown Park area.
Operating from January 1921 through May 1997, the
store offered shoes, boots, tennis shoes, orthopedic
corrections and repairing for 76 years.
*(Submitted by Chris Holubar Walsh and
Francine Rhodes, daughters of Joseph Holubar Jr.)*

Printers for the Generations

In 1927 Barnhart Press shows off a new printing press. The business, on 13th between Howard and Harney Streets was owned and operated then by Clairbel Foster Barnhart (third from left) and John W. Barnhart (fourth from the left). Barnhart Press moved to its present location at 26th and Farnam Streets in 1940. Third- and fourth-generation Barnhart and Caulk family members now run the business.

(Submitted by Janet Barnhart Caulk, granddaughter of John and Clairbel Barnhart)

Graduation at St. Philomena's

The 1929 graduating class of St. Philomena's School, 16th and Leavenworth Streets. Top row (left to right): Sam Curro, Paul Sapienzia, Josephine Gerompini, Helen White (fifth from left), Bill Heaston, Joe Luccino and Tony Portera. Bottom row (second from left): Helen Farhat, Alice Guard, Josephine Ferris (fifth from left) and Mary Simiho.
(Submitted by Louise R. Portera, wife of Tony Portera)

Pro Pitcher

John C. Braniff and his sister, Pearl Braniff Starkey, in 1929. John was a champion pitcher for the Omaha Browns and played professional baseball for the St. Louis Browns. His wife, Rose, wanted him to remain in Omaha, so John retired from baseball and worked as the manager for Mother's Best Flowers.
(Submitted by Frank Peters, nephew of John Braniff)

A Day in the Peony Pool

From left, Sally Robison, Conrad Young, May Scotland Young, Peggy Young and Bonnie Young and an unidentified friend, at Peony Park in 1929.

(Submitted by Conrad Young)

Fleet of Five

The Nash Cab Co. fleet in 1929. The firm's office was at 4426 S. 24th St. Fourth from left is employee Clark Huxtable.

(Submitted by Carol S. Edmunds, Clark's daughter)

Benson Showplace

Bernice Corbaley and her brother, Lewis, at the fish pond in their back yard. Their father, J.L. Corbaley, had a fondness for fish ponds, so he built one at his home, 2943 N. 58th St., in 1930. J.L. owned Corbaley Shoe Store, 6013 Maple St., in Benson. *(Submitted by Nancy Lindell Leslie, J.L.'s granddaughter)*

Hand-to-Horn Combat

Pappy Ryan bulldogging at the Omaha Rodeo in the early 1930s at Ak-Sar-Ben. Ak-Sar-Ben has done a Livestock Show since 1927 and a rodeo the past 53 years. *(Submitted by Burnice Fiedler)*

Farris Haberdashery

Thomas Farris at his Farris Haberdashery at 24th and M Streets during the 1930s. He operated the business for five years. During the Great Depression, the business closed, and Farris went to work for the city.
(Submitted by Joan Farris Ellis, Farris' daughter)

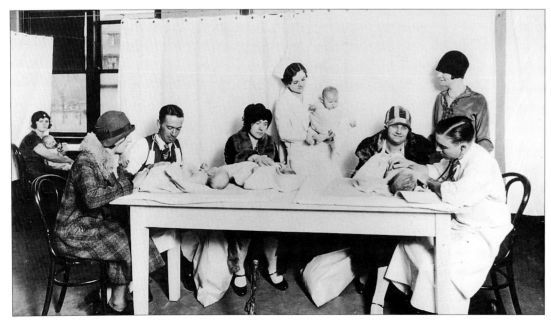

Baby Exams at University

Infants undergo checkups at University Hospital.
(Submitted by Nebraska Health System)

Archer and Architect

Architect Thomas R. Kimball (far left) on an archery and golf outing at the Omaha Country Club in 1930. *(Submitted by Tom Kohoutek)*

Softball at Falstaff Park

Teams meet in the 1944 State Softball Tournament at Falstaff Park, 24th and Vinton Streets. Falstaff Park was built in May 1936 and was the official park of the Nebraska State Softball Association. In the years before World War II, more than 3,500 fans would turn out for games there. During the war, attendance dropped, and the park closed in 1949. It was torn down a year later. *(Submitted by Jim Borowiak, whose father, Paul Borowiak, owned the field for several years)*

Chance Encounter

William McDonnell meets President Herbert Hoover and his wife, Lou, at an Omaha train depot in 1932. McDonnell was delivering milk for the Fairmont Creamery and recognized Sen. Malcolm Baldrige, R-Neb., in the president's entourage. Baldrige, an Omahan, called McDonnell, with whom he had worked years before, to the president's car. Hoover was campaigning for re-election. He lost heavily in November to Franklin D. Roosevelt. *(Submitted by Tim Bernet, William's great-grandson)*

Plucking for Campbell's

Workers remove pinfeathers from chickens at the Campbell's Soup plant, 12th and Douglas Streets, in the late 1930s. *(Submitted by Michael Hetherington)*

Grocery Store Trade-Off

Tom Nastase (second from left) worked at A. Marino Grocery, 1716 S. 13th St., in 1931 for $15 per week. When he married the daughter of his boss, Andrew Marino (left), he was provided an apartment above the store to live in. His pay, however, was decreased to $10 per week. The grocery store remains in business today and is known for its homemade Italian sausage.

(Submitted by Tom Nastase Jr.)

When Refrigerators Were Rare

The ice house and filling station at 3517 S. 32nd Ave., was operated by Joe Bell. It stood next to Bell and Laferla Groceries. Joe is shown with his wife, Maria. Maria never missed a day of bringing Joe a hot meal at lunch time. Both pictures were taken in 1932.

(Submitted by Mary Laferla Rook, granddaughter of Joe and Maria)

The Journeyman Printer

Robert Gilder at his studio home known as Wake Robin, situated in woods near Bellevue Boulevard and Grove Road, in 1931. A New York native, Gilder came to Omaha in 1886 to work as a printer, typesetter, proofreader, reporter and editor. He spent most of his working years at The World-Herald and described himself as a "journeyman printer." In retirement, he devoted himself to painting and other hobbies. The University of Nebraska awarded him an honorary degree for his discovery of eight ancient skulls north of Hummel Park.
(Submitted by George Kieser)

U.S.S. Omahan

William R. Pixley (foreground, far left) in class with his naval mates in July 1932. Pixley was the only Omahan on the U.S.S. Omaha.
(Submitted by Patricia Pixley, William's daughter-in-law)

Grocers to the Neighborhood

From left: Jim, John, Ida, Angeline, Joe and Mary Laferla at Bell and Laferla Groceries, 3517 S. 32nd Ave., in 1932. The family owned the store until father John retired in 1952, and it served as a neighborhood hub during the summer. The area is now part of Interstate 480.
(Submitted by Mary Laferla Rook)

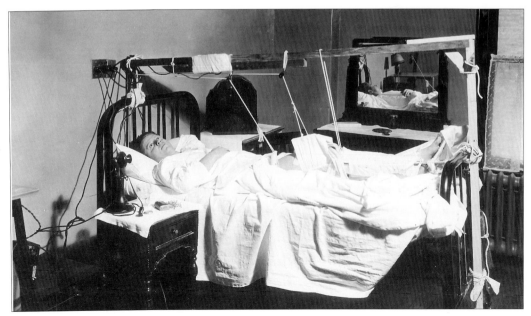

Recovering at Lord Lister

Clyde Drew Jr. recovers in the Lord Lister private hospital at 14th Street and Capitol Avenue in February 1933.
(Submitted by Jack Drew)

Cudahy Packers

The beef casing department at Cudahy Packing Co., 33rd and L Streets, Oct. 17, 1933. Second row, eighth from left is Joseph Pawlowicz. *(Submitted by Rudy and Rita Stoysich; Joseph is Rita's father)*

A Budding Businessman

A photographer captures three-year-old Benjamin Wiesman in front of Evans Grocery Store, 3522 N. 16th St., in 1934. Samuel Wiesman was proprietor of the store. Ben went on to play a part in establishing many of the call centers in the nation, including Micor at 7720 Crown Point Ave., which took hotel reservations. The building was the first reservation center designed from the ground up. *(Submitted by Ben Wiesman, Samuel's son)*

The Big Day

Carl and Mary Boehm were married July 28, 1934, at St. Bernard Catholic Church, 3604 N. 65th St. Also pictured are wedding party members Ann Barr, left, Leslie Kulhanek, third from left, and Lillian Barr, right. Carl "Dutch" Boehm worked in The World-Herald composing room until his death in 1971. *(Submitted by Darlene Hodakowski, daughter of Carl and Mary)*

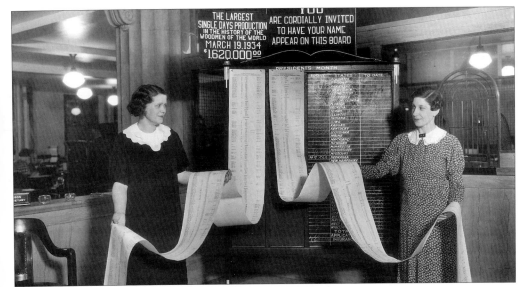

A Woodmen Record

Louise Kammenzind (left) and Rose Rubin of Woodmen of the World Life Insurance Society display the tally of the Woodmen's largest single day of insurance sales. The record day, March 19, 1934, was achieved during "President's Month," a sales promotion recognizing National President De Emmett Bradshaw's 35 years of Woodmen service. *(Submitted by Woodmen of the World)*

Queen for a Day

Dolores Westbrook was named queen of the Baby Beauty and Health Contest, conducted by Roosevelt Post No. 30 of the American Legion in 1934. The show included baby health examinations, a baby beauty show and the coronation of a baby king and queen. *(Submitted by Donna Abusin)*

Nurses of the Challenger

Mae Brogan (left) was a registered nurse who assisted passengers on Union Pacific's The Challenger between Omaha, Denver, and San Francisco. The Challenger was popular with travelers, especially women and children, because of the nurses. Mae worked until she got married in 1940. The picture was taken in 1935. *(Submitted by Kathleen Hughes, daughter of Mae Brogan Hughes)*

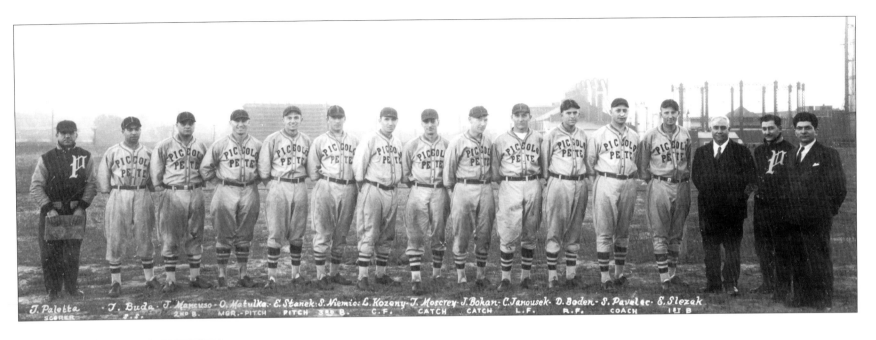

J. Paletta · J. Buda · J. Mancuso · O. Matulka · E. Stanek · S. Niemic · L. Kozeny · T. Moscrey · J. Bohan · C. Janousek · D. Boden · S. Pavelec · E. Slezak
SCORER   S.S.   2ND B.   MGR.-PITCH PITCH 3RD B.   C.F.   CATCH   CATCH   L.F.   R.F.   COACH   1ST B.

Piccolo's Players

The Piccolo Pete's baseball team of 1935, metro champions that year. From left: J. Paletta, J. Buda, J. Mancuso, O. Matulka, E. Stanek, S. Niemic, L. Kozeny, T. Moscrey, J. Bohan, C. Janousek, D. Boden, S. Pavelec, E. Slezak, J. Piccolo, A.J. Piccolo, A. Monaco.
(Submitted by Nadine Graves and Donna Sheehan)

Where Little Italy Shopped

Subby Piccolo, in front of Piccolo Pete's grocery store, Sixth and Pierce Streets, in 1935. Piccolo Pete's was started by Joseph Piccolo in the 1920s as a grocery store. In 1934, Joseph started the tavern Piccolo Pete's at 2202 S. 20th Street with his son Tony. Piccolo Pete's is now a restaurant.
(Submitted by Gary Domet, nephew of Subby and Tony and grandson of Joseph).

Mormons Remember

The monument to the pioneers who died at the Mormons' winter encampment in 1846-47 is dedicated in Florence on Sept. 20, 1936.
(Submitted by Jack Drew)

Republican Rally

Alf Landon, governor of Kansas and Republican candidate for president in 1936, appears at a rally in front of the Hotel Fontenelle at 18th and Douglas Streets.
(Submitted by Jack Drew)

The Humane Society

A view of the Humane Society at 924 N. 21st St. in 1936. Sarah Joslyn hired Clyde W. Drew Sr. to run the society that same year. *(Submitted by Jack Drew)*

Friend to the Animals

Charles Davey in front of his Humane Society truck in the early 1920s. Charles served as a blacksmith and groundskeeper for Sarah Joslyn, who funded Omaha's first animal humane society. Having cared for the animals at the Joslyn home, Charles was appointed as Omaha's first animal protection officer. *(Submitted by Charles Davey, grandson of Charles)*

Confirmation Day at St. Therese

Confirmation is celebrated at St. Therese of the Child Jesus Catholic Church, 1423 Ogden St. The photo was taken about 1936. The robed adult celebrants are, from left, Monsignor Patrick A. Flanagan, pastor of Holy Angels; Father James J. O'Brien, pastor of St. Therese; Bishop James H. Ryan; and Monsignor Edward Burke, pastor of St. Philip Neri.

(Submitted by Mary Agnes Smith)

Red Perkins Band

The Red Perkins Band performed at the Dreamland Ballroom, 24th and Grant Streets, in the 1930s. Jessie Pluke Simmons (second from right in foreground) played the alto saxophone.
(Submitted by Leella Payne, niece of Jessie Pluke Simmons)

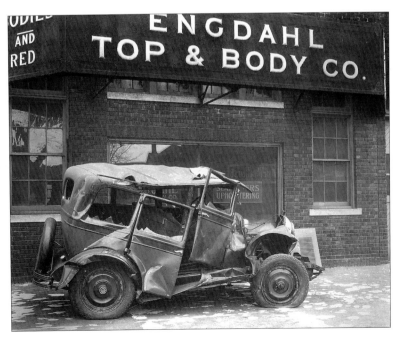

In Business Since 1916

John S. Engdahl opened Engdahl Top and Body Shop, 614 N. 18th St., in 1916 and operated the business until his retirement in 1974. The photo was taken around 1930. The shop included a full woodworking area and upholstery shop, and it specialized in building armored cars, ambulances and limousines. John's son Rodney Engdahl, continues to operate the business today.
(Submitted by John L. Engdahl, John S.'s grandson)

24th and Ames

The intersection of 24th Street and Ames Avenue in 1936. *(Submitted by Mrs. Byron E. "June" Palmer)*

On the Bread Run

From 1935 to 1966, Stanley Nabb worked for Omar Bakeries, in Omaha and other cities. Pictured here is his delivery wagon from the early years of his job. Every morning, Nabb would load the wagon with bread and sweet goods. He would hitch up the horse to deliver to homes in the Morton Meadows area from 42nd Street to Saddle Creek Road and from Pierce to Pine Streets. His horse knew the route and how to read the stoplights. While Nabb made deliveries, the horse would move to the end of the block and wait for him. In 1938, Nabb switched to a truck. It took him an hour longer each day to complete his route.
(Submitted by Stanley Nabb)

Coffee Shop Courtship

Helen Kalina (behind counter) at work at the G & G Coffee Shop, 13th and Farnam Streets, inside the Merchants National Bank, in 1937. It was there she met the owner's son, Earl Zentz Jr. whom she later married. The shop was owned by Earl Sr. and Hazel Zentz.
(Submitted by Earl and Helen Kalina Zentz)

Making Tracks

Ernest Brunn built this model train for his son, Dick, in 1937. From left, Dick, his sister Malvina and two neighbor friends watch the train circle the track in the basement of the Brunn home at 4418 Farnam St. For years, Dick added to his train collection, which he still has today.
(Submitted by Malvina Brunn Stephens)

Milder Oil Meeting

William Green, seated on the far right at the front left table, attends a Milder Oil Co. sales meeting at the Paxton Hotel Dec. 6, 1937. Green was a personal friend of Hymie Milder, president of the company. Green was the county surveyor from 1936 to 1939, worked at Union Pacific until 1947 and served as city commissioner until 1951. He was elected again to county surveyor in 1951 and served until his death in 1958. When he died, his nephew by the same name was awarded the right to run for the office and won.

(Submitted by John Thomas Green, son of William Green)

Happy Birthday 2 You

Children sing "Happy Birthday" to Shirley Farquhar, standing to right of the cake stand, who turns 2, at St. Paul Methodist Church, 54th and Corby Streets, on Nov. 1, 1937.

(Submitted by Robert Farquhar, Shirley's brother)

Passover Dinner

From left, Bess, Julius, Larry, Bessi, Sam, Kiva, Ida and Helen Hornstein, Dorothy Blau and Joe Hornston gather at Sam and Bessi's home at 20th and Binney Streets to observe Passover in 1937. *(Submitted by Martha Mason Frishman, Helen's daughter)*

A Star is Born

Father Edward Flanagan welcomes Spencer Tracy, left, and Mickey Rooney to Boys Town in 1938 for the premiere of the movie "Boys Town." *(Submitted by Girls and Boys Town Hall of History)*

Soccer and Suds

Sixth from right, Charlie Nanfito played soccer for the Hamm's Beer Team in 1938. The team took the city championship in the Omaha recreation soccer league that year. Soccer teams were all sponsored by the local breweries.

(Submitted by Meg Nanfito Jones, Charlie's daughter)

Shave and a Haircut

John Vaculik (front, cutting hair in 1939) owned a barber shop at the Delmar Hotel, 24th and Farnam Streets. He worked as a barber for more than 40 years and after retirement filled in for vacationing barbers.
(Submitted by Marjorie Vaculik, daughter-in-law of John Vaculik)

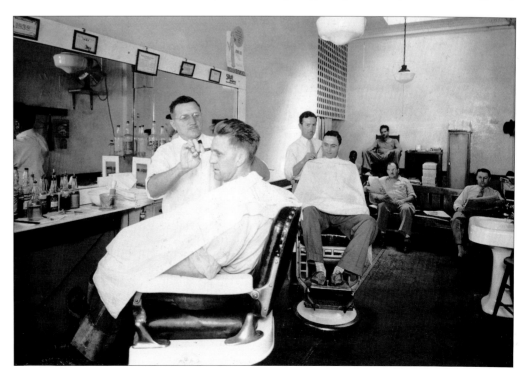

They've Got Rhythm

District 25 was a one-room school, located at 150th Street and West Dodge Road. Pictured here is the District 25 rhythm band in 1939, composed of the entire student body. Back row (from left): Pauline Travis, Dorothy Stolley, Harriet Penke, teacher Helen Kranbeck, Yvonne Travis, Marjorie Stolley and Peggy Kuehl. Bottom row: Barbara Dau, Ramona Wollen, Bobby Willmer and Tommy Brozek.
(Submitted by Marjorie Stolley Vaculik)

On Stage at Peony Park

The Sparta Orchestra at Peony Park in 1939. From row from left: Jerry Jaros, Bill Brown, Frank Jaros and Bob Kafka. Back row from left: Ed Julius, Paul Rada and John Julius.
(Submitted by Patti Slama, daughter of John Julius)

Mutual Builds a Home

In 1939, at 33rd and Farnam Streets, cornerstone ceremonies are held for the first building owned by Mutual of Omaha. The company had previously leased space in several downtown buildings. Mutual Benefit Health and Accident Association was started in 1909 by Dr. C.C. and Mabel Criss. The company changed its name to Mutual of Omaha Insurance Co. in 1962. V. J. Skutt, who served as Mutual's chairman and chief executive officer, from 1953-1984, is pictured addressing the crowd.

(Submitted by Mutual of Omaha)

Golden Spike Parade
The Golden Spike Days parade in 1939 on 15th Street between Harney and Farnam.

(Submitted by John Yirak)

A Saloon Keeper on Parade

Eddie Guziac (left) takes the reins in front of his bar, the Polonia, 24th and M Streets, during Golden Spike Days in April 1939. As a marketing promotion, Hamm's Beer provided the wagon for Eddie to ride in the Golden Spike parade through the parade. *(Submitted by Barbara A. Costello, Eddie's daughter)*

Prairie Lasses

The first Golden Spike Days celebration took place in April 1939. A second celebration followed in 1940. Dressed for the occasion are back row, from left Elsa Swanson, Eva Swanson, Lillie Dahlgren and Ruth Swanson. In the front row are Nancy Dahlgren, left, and Shirley Swanson. *(Submitted by Eva Swanson)*

Crinoline Days

Charlie Maxwell and his daughters, Bonnie (left) and Mary Beth, performed the song "Back to the Crinoline Days" on the radio and at the Union Pacific Railroad during Golden Spike Days in 1939. Bonnie and Mary Beth sang, and Charlie played piano. *(Submitted by Bonnie Maxwell Pryor)*

Not His Auto Service Uniform

O.A. Dahlgren, left, and a Mr. Wright as they decked themselves out for Golden Spike Days in 1939. Dahlgren owned American Auto Service at 1116 Jackson St. *(Submitted by Nancy Dahlgren, O.A.'s daughter).*

The Golden Spike Look

Fake store fronts were placed in front of Kilpatrick's and other downtown businesses near 15th and Douglas Streets during Golden Spike Days in April 1939.

(Submitted by Omaha Community Playhouse)

That's Right – Golden Spike Days

The Kirk family poses for a picture at the Shamrock Club, 5212 S. 25th St., during Golden Spike Days in 1939. From left, Minnie, Colleen, Jessie Ford Kirk, Lacy G. Kirk, Lacy M. Kirk Sr. and James Kirk. The club was owned by Jessie's parents, Jim and Minnie Ford.

(Submitted by Michael Kirk)

Orchard & Wilhelm Store

Storewide Enthusiasm

Employees at Orchard and Wilhelm Home Furnishings, 16th and Howard Streets, celebrate Golden Spike Days in 1939. Iver Ahrenkiel, the store's appliance department manager, is among the group.
(Submitted by Frances Rosholm Ahrenkiel, Iver's widow)

Pioneer Printers

The office and sales staff of Peterson Lithograph and Printing Co. (later known as United States Checkbook Co.) during Golden Spike Days in 1939.
(Submitted by Cathy Dempsey)

The Family That Plays Together...

From left: Dick, Leonard and Eddie Janak with their father Peter (holding saxophone) in 1939. Peter taught music to the three sons. The sons each became leaders of their own orchestras and often entertained at Sokol Hall, 13th and Martha Streets; Bethsaida Hall, 25th and Seward Streets; and the Peony Park ballroom, as well as other dance halls.
(Submitted by Lee Janak, Dick's wife)

Picnic in the Park

Dudley Round and his son, Jack, and daughter, Marianne, on a bridge at Hummel Park in 1939 during a picnic outing.
(Submitted by Sharon Weak, daughter of Dudley)

At the Doll Family Farm

The Doll family at their farm in 1940, near today's intersection of 108th Street and West Center Road. Back row, from left: Marie Kocher Doll, Emil, Ann, Albert, Frank, Ella, George, Myrtle and Robert Doll. Front row, from left: Richard, Ivan, Donald, Virginia, Laura, Augustus, Bob, Lyle, Merlin and Elden Doll. *(Submitted by Richard Doll, Augustus' grandson)*

Who Brought the Food?

Jacob Schmid (standing, third from left) attends the Grocers and Butchers Association annual picnic at Vennelyst Park in Florence in the 1940s. Jacob owned and ran Schmid Meat Market at 2128 N. 16th St. for more than 50 years. *(Submitted by Jean Schmid, daughter-in-law of Jacob)*

Best Lemonade in Benson

This Benson lemonade stand was a spur-of-the-moment idea for these young entrepreneurs in the early 1940s. From left, Shirley Grogan, Nancy Wurgler, Tom Grogan and Bill Wurgler. They sold the lemonade in front of a grocery store and a dentist's office at 51st Street and Military Avenue. The bucket of lemonade sits on two orange crates that cost a total of a nickel. Tom later used the crates to make Soap Box Derby cars.
(Submitted by Shirley Grogan Gouger)

Line Repair

A streetcar repair truck on the job at 22nd and Nicholas Streets in 1940.
(Submitted by Mrs. Byron E. "June" Palmer)

First, It Was the World

The scene outside the Omaha Theater, 15th and Douglas Streets, in the early 1940s. Originally called the World Theater and designed by architect Harry Lawrie, it opened in 1922. It seated 2,500 and was built for both vaudeville and motion pictures. It became the Omaha Theater in 1935. It closed in 1978.

(Submitted by Joan Calandra Swan)

Ready to Serve

A group of 1950 employees at Johnny's Cafe, 4702 S. 27th St. *(Submitted by Mary Kawa, daugher-in-law of John Kawa, the cafe's founder)*

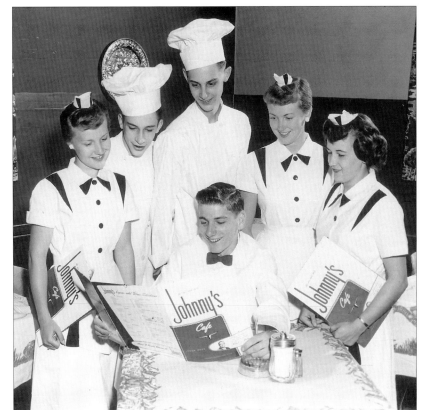

There's Nothing Like Hamm's on a Hot Day

From left, Emily Schonlau, Dorothy Albrecht, Orville Albrecht and William Schonlau pose for an advertising shot for Hamm's Beer at Vennelyst Park in Florence, July 12, 1940. *(Submitted by Barbara Lokke, Emily and William's daughter).*

Stolinski Livestock Exchange

Ted Stolinski Sr., the son of Polish immigrants, started as an office boy at the livestock building, but was required—by doctor's orders—to work outside because of the heavy smoke inside. Although he was scared to death of animals, he worked outside and learned the business. In 1928 he opened Stolinski Livestock Exchange, a livestock commission business. After Stolinski's death in 1948, his sons Art and Ted Jr. took over the business. From left: Art Stolinski, Jim "Jazzy" Melady (on horse), Leo Augustine, and Ted Stolinkski Jr.

(Submitted by Mary K. Stolinski, Ted Sr.'s daughter)

Crack-Ups

During the 1940s, Louise Portera and her co-workers cracked eggs for C.A. Swanson and Sons. The company made powdered eggs for the armed services and shipped them overseas.
(Submitted by Louise R. Portera)

Brighten Your Day

Started by the Nebraska Power Co. and continued by its successor company, OPPD, the Lamp Counter was operated until 1970. From left, Lucille Quackenbush and Jo Horn sold light bulbs and electric appliance accessories on the first floor of the Electric Building. This photo was taken in the days of the Nebraska Power Co.
(Submitted by Omaha Public Power District)

An Early Drive-In

The B-26 Drive-In at 24th Street and Deer Park Boulevard in the late 1940s. In 1953, the B-26 became the Sperry LeRoy restaurant; later various bars were located in the building. *(Submitted by Louis Marcuzzo)*

Lab Work

The Clarkson Hospital laboratory. *(Submitted by Nebraska Health System)*

At the Music Box

Jane Griffith (on violin) and her Rhythm Queens All Girl Orchestra perform at the Music Box, 19th Street and Capitol Avenue. The orchestra, including Mary Lou Brunson on drums and Jean Price (the middle trumpet player), performed at the Paxton Hotel, Fontenelle Hotel, the Central Club and other places during the 1940s. They were billed as the Midwest's only all-girl band.

(Submitted by Mary Lou Brunson)

Friendships Live On

Following World War II, many men who had formed friendships before the war congregated at uniform parties, held at Terry's Swing Spot on South 10th Street. In order to attend, the men were required to wear their uniforms, which represented every branch of the service. At later parties, some of the uniforms did not fit as well, so the men fastened them with rubber bands and safety pins, adding to the fun.
(Submitted by retired Judge Patrick W. Lynch, among those pictured)

John - Ray - Hank
Marchello Marchello Sansone

Ollie Marshal - Babe Downs Carl - Seb - Gildo - Bill - Ag. Jim - Frank - Lou - Sam - ? - Diz - Terry
Distefano Aliano Cortese Lindsay Wolf DiLorenzo Piccolo D'Agosta Melingagi Distefano Panebianco

Tony Seb - Anthony
Catalano Turco - "Cookie" Salerno - Nate Distefano - Tange Marcuccio

Tom "Muleph" Vitale Spike Distefano - Gus - Frank - Bernie John Frank Seb
Polito Sneboda Bisbee LaMantia Maggio Noble

Jim Lynch - J."Doggie" Vitale - Al Angele Terry - Tony Miloni - Chuck
Manganaro Farraguti

"Danny? -Pat Lynch - Pete Rasmussen -? Chas Anxalone - J. "Jeep" Ferrara Tom Gillogly - Sam Caniglia Paul Garroto
Vince Catalano Joe "Chickens" Campagna

Wartime Toy Drive

From left: Elizabeth Murphy, Mary Louis Stash, Margaret Dwyer, Mary Provaznik, Margaret Stover, Alice McGowan and Jean Rerucha were members of Kappa Zeta Kappa sorority at Creighton University in the spring of 1942. The organization gathered at Margaret Stover's home, 118 S. 52nd St., to assemble toys for families of men in the military service. John Popa, a Creighton journalism student, took the picture.
(Submitted by Margaret Dwyer Dutch)

Joining the Faithful at St. Cecilia

St. Cecilia Cathedral, First Holy Communion, May 18, 1941. Father George Kempker (back, left) was the assistant pastor; he later founded St. Pius X Catholic Church. Molly Finney (first row, fifth from right) and Bonnie Maxwell (second row, seventh from left) stayed involved at St. Cecilia's. Molly is St. Cecilia school secretary and Bonnie is the principal.
(Submitted by Bonnie Maxwell Pryor)

Marie and Her Harley

Marie Christensen on her 1938 Harley Knucklehead motorcycle at Riverview Park in 1942. Crocodiles would lie on the banks of the water near the bridge in the background, and people would feed them. Henry Doorly Zoo now occupies the land.

(Submitted by Marie Christensen)

He Gave His Life

During World War II, Walter Buras trained Creighton University students from the Army Air Corps to become pilots. During a training session at the Omaha Municipal Airport in 1943, Walter and a student pilot were killed. *(Submitted by Tom Buras, cousin of Walter)*

Christmas Contributions

During World War II, Carmen Frolio Grasso was a final assembly inspector at the Martin Bomber Plant near Bellevue (where Offutt Air Force Base now stands). Here, she hangs coins on a display at the plant. The coins were used to purchase "smokes for the boys overseas." *(Submitted by Carmen F. Grasso)*

Ready to Serve

During World War II, the Red Cross offered a training course for canteen workers. In October 1943, this group of women successfully completed the course and went on to serve at canteens for servicemen. From left: Mabel Anderson, Alta Weymuller, Mary Claire Wall, Inez Mortensen, Beatrice Chalupnik, Mildred Martins and Mary Majors. *(Submitted by Mrs. C.H. Dunn, pictured on the far right)*

Pressed Into Service

The small boat in the foreground, built and used by Ray Rosholm and Iver Ahrenkiel, assists the Army Corps of Engineers during the flooding of the Omaha Municipal Airport, Carter Lake and nearby areas in April 1943.

(Submitted by Frances Rosholm Ahrenkiel, sister of Ray and widow of Iver).

Jamming at the Junior Bar

Jess Busse, right, and his wife, Ann, perform at the Junior Bar, 414 N. 16th St., in 1945. Jess and his brothers were all musical: Fred played piano, Burt played the fiddle and Jess played trumpet.
(Submitted by Andre H. and Elizabeth Busse; Andre is Jess' nephew)

Motor Men

From left are: Pete Pecha, with sons (from left) Ron, Don and John, in 1944. Cars have been a part of the boys' life since childhood. John went on to own Benson Radiator Service at 7059 Maple St. His wife, Kathy, still owns the shop. Ron and his sons race at Sunset Speedway, and Don is a mechanic.
(Submitted by Denise Pecha, daughter of Don Pecha)

Graduating Angels

May 1945 kindergarten graduation at Holy Angels School, 28th Street and Fowler Avenue. Top row (left to right): Diane Anderson, Steve Morrow, Jean Blair (fourth from left) Marceline Aurora, Maurine Boaner, Jim McKinney, Rosie Murray (ninth from left), Marlene Schmitz and Lois Johnson. Middle row (left to right): Johnny Vernilli (third from left), Tim Manion, Jerry Hart, David Smith, Maurice Berry, Barb Reynek (ninth from left), Kathy Galloway, Loraine Luce, Mary Ortman, Allen Johnson and Rosemary Messing. Bottom row (left to right): Virginia Hansen, Pete Costello, Lynn McGuire, Mary McCafferty, Lorretta Kearney, Joan Mack (eighth from left), David Morrow and Jim Watsabaugh.

(Submitted by Mary Nastase, one of the graduates)

113

On the Home Front

During World War II, while many men in the company's work force were in the military, Cora Rigg and other women drove trucks for Omar Bakeries. This picture was taken in 1945. From left, Jean Hamilton, Cora Rigg, Beulah Zimmerman, Molly Zimmerman, Marie Anderson, Elmer Swanson, Toadie Rinehardt, Nancy Fried, Bonnie Mahon and Margaret Beck.

(Submitted by Susan M. Thomas, granddaughter of Cora Rigg)

Christmas at the Chief

A crowd gathers in front of the Chief Theatre, 24th and K Streets, for a Christmas party sponsored by KMTV in 1947. When the theater opened in 1941, it boasted of the "newest ultra-modern innovations," including pushback seats, a crying room for babies, an ice cream bar, air conditioning and hearing aids.
(Submitted by Leslie Babendir)

Movies and Matrimony

During the 1940s, Abe Cohn, managed the Chief Theatre at 24th and K Streets. He also oversaw weddings held there. The theater seated over 1,200 people and was open from 1941 through 1972.
(Submitted by Leslie Babendir, Abe's niece)

West Sisters String Quartet

The West Sisters String Quartet entertained at Sunday afternoon teas for the wealthy in the Gold Coast neighborhood from before 1920 and through the 1930s. Sarah Joslyn was one of the quartet's patrons. They performed on Omaha's first radio station, WAOW. Eloise and Madge West were among the first members of the Omaha Symphony and performed with the orchestra into the 1950s. From left, Madge, Vivienne, Eloise and Belle West in the 1920s. *(Submitted by Wm. L. McNichols, son of Eloise West McNichols)*

"Fast, Complete Service"

Sandy Italia (pumping gas) took over the Skelly service station at 40th and Dodge Streets in December 1947. "Fast, complete service," was Sandy's motto. He recruited part-time workers for the station from local schools and universities. At the time he took over the station, gas sold for 19.9 cents per gallon. One employee was Eugene Leahy, Omaha's mayor from 1969-73. *(Submitted by Mrs. Sandy Italia)*

Knights of the Ice

The 1946-1947 Omaha Knights hockey team.
The team drew big crowds at Ak-Sar-Ben.
(Submitted by Louie Marcuzzo)

A Future Annie Oakley

Lenore Baburek poses on a traveling pony
at 2739 S. 13th St. in the late '40s.
(Submitted by Lenore Deeths)

Clerks of the Phillip's Store

Joyce Rice, fifth from left, worked as a sales clerk for the Phillip's Store at 24th and O Streets, when this photo was taken in 1948. Joyce went on to marry Melvin Mladovich and resigned from her job at the store.

(Submitted by Greg and Mary Mladovich, son and daughter-in-law of Melvin and Joyce)

The Successful Type

Lacy G. Kirk started Kirk's Typewriter Co., 2420 M St., in 1939. Lacy, left, is shown with his son, James L. Kirk, in 1947. The business is still open today.
(*Submitted by Michael Kirk, grandson of Lacy G. Kirk*)

Later, He Became Mayor

For over 30 years, Bernie Simon installed telephones for Northwestern Bell Co. Both he and his wife were employed there in 1948 when this picture was taken. Bernie later became a city councilman and was mayor of Omaha from Feb. 6, 1987 to April 13, 1988.
(*Submitted by Curt Simon, son of Bernie*)

Caught in the Act

From left, Alan Severin, Paul Simpkins and John McKenzie play at the closed Krug Park swimming pool (now Gallagher Park), 52nd and Maple Streets, in 1948. During that time, polio scares convinced many parents to declare the pool area off-limits to their children. When their parents would ask whether they had been there, the boys would answer, "no." This picture was published in The World-Herald, including the names of each child, confirming they were at the pool. The children confessed.

(Submitted by Alan Severin)

Trentino's Cafe

Trentino's Cafe, at 10th and Pacific Streets (now Angie's), was open every day but Tuesday until 1 a.m. A group of co-workers and friends gathered for this photo in 1948. Seated from left, Lorraine Lakin, Mary Firmature and Antoinette. Standing from left: Louise Salerno, Sam Firmature, Billie Thompson, Marian Covich, unknown, Cathy Narmi and Norma Pattavina. They were all friends who worked together at the restaurant.
(Submitted by Charlotte Covich Young, daughter of Marian Covich)

All Aboard for Bible School

In 1949, this cut-out sign was constructed by Carl Lindell to encourage children to attend vacation bible school at Third Presbyterian Church, 20th and Leavenworth Streets. Carl owned a sign shop in Ralston from 1955-1992. Ronald Swain (far left), Cheryl Longacre (third from left), Nancy Lindell (fifth from left) and John Emery (seventh from left) stand in front of the sign.
(Submitted by Nancy Lindell Leslie, daughter of Carl)

121

Leader of the Navy

Omahan Francis P. Matthews (on the left) is welcomed by Secretary of Defense Louis Johnson as the new secretary of the Navy in May 1949. With Matthews are members of his family, from left, Matthews, Patricia, Mary Claire, Francis, Mrs. Matthews, Kathleen, Marguerite Matthews Snyder and Marian. Matthews later became the U.S. ambassador to Ireland, a post he held at the time of his death of a heart attack, while visiting Omaha in 1952. *(Submitted by Kathleen Matthews Irvine)*

The Hruska Kids Mount Up

A traveling photographer captured the Hruska siblings in front of their home at 5638 S. 20th St. in the summer of 1949. Pictured are Ed (standing) and from left, Margaret, Tom and Mary.
(Submitted by the Hruska family)

Union Pacific Sports Club

The Union Pacific Sports Club was started by U.P. employees to enjoy sports, dances and parties. Here the club holds a ping pong tournament at the YMCA, 17th Street and St. Mary's Avenue, in 1949. Members Lois and Don Smith and Dorothy Wild and Howard Sowl are pictured in the backgroud.

(Submitted by Dorothy Sowl)

Love Story

In the spring of 1949, Union Pacific Sports Club member Dorothy Wild (pictured in the checkered dress in the background) was asked to skate by fellow member Howard Sowl at the Crosstown Roller Rink at 24th and Leavenworth Streets. She met him a second time at the Ak-Sar-Ben Skating Rink in the winter of 1949 and they were married in March of 1951.

(Submitted by Dorothy Sowl)

Help for Homemakers

OPPD's Home Service Director Alice Ward and a WOW radio announcer await a girl's approval as she samples whipped frosting during a broadcast of "Homemakers Club of the Air." Members of the Home Service Department were regarded as the area's cooking experts. Homemakers, nursing students, restaurant owners, grocers, widowers, school teachers and Scout groups were among those who looked to the department for answers to questions ranging from cooking to canning to cleaning.
(Submitted by Omaha Public Power District)

Keeping Omaha Wired

Line dispatchers once manually controlled the flow of power over the miles of circuits serving OPPD customers. John Foraker, left, and Ken Robinson are shown on the job in the 1950s.
(Submitted by Omaha Public Power District)

Where Santa Reigned

The animated Christmas display on the eighth floor of the Brandeis Store, 16th and Douglas Streets, got bigger and better every year. Here, Catherine Lynn asks Santa for a Betsy Wetsy doll in 1950. The Korean War had begun earlier that year, and it was difficult to purchase goods made of rubber. Catherine's mother had a friend who was a teacher. The teacher secured a second-hand doll for Catherine from one of her students. Her mother eventually was able to buy Catherine a new doll. *(Submitted by Catherine Lynn)*

Christmas Wishes

Diann Hofmann in front of the large southwest show window at the Brandeis Store a few days before Christmas in 1949. There was high anticipation each year to see the new Christmas displays at Brandeis. Christmas was not complete without visiting Santa on the eighth floor. *(Submitted by Mary Lou Brunson, Diann's mom)*

Grand Opening

Calandra Camera Co.'s second retail store at 24th and N Streets had its grand opening in 1948. An Italian immigrant, Bernard A. Calandra founded the company in 1936 with a savings of $2,000, and it grew to include locations in Nebraska, New Mexico, Colorado, Kansas, North and South Dakota, Missouri, Iowa, Minnesota, Wyoming and Texas. Bernard's sons took over the business after he died in 1957. The business was sold to Fox Photo in 1972. *(Submitted by the Calandra Family)*

Donations for Santa Lucia

Joseph Piccolo adds donated money to the Santa Lucia decorations at St. Philomena Catholic Church, 10th and William Streets, during the 1950s. The church is now St. Frances Cabrini and the festival lives on. *(Submitted by Nadine Graves and Donna Sheehan, granddaughters of Joseph)*

Man With a Horn

Donnie Kelly played trombone with the Preston Love Orchestra during the 1950s. The group traveled and performed throughout the nation. *(Submitted by Donna Abusin, daughter of Kelly)*

"House Party" Winner

Anna Hruza poses for a promotional photograph with an AirWay Sanitizor vacuum cleaner in her home at 5117 S. 19th St. Anna won the vacuum after mailing in a contest entry for Art Linkletter's "House Party" television program in the early 1950s. *(Submitted by Mary Brau, daughter of Anna)*

At the Douglas Street Bridge

Frank Schultz, spent over 30 years on the Missouri River, running a fishery consisting of a tiny cottage, several old boats, worn nets and a battered dock. He sold carp, buffalo and catfish, fresh from the river. Here he is in front of the old Douglas Street bridge. The Interstate 480 bridge now stands in its place today. *(Submitted by William E. Ramsey)*

Ready to Go

The Benson fire station at 60th and Maple Streets in the 1940s. *(Submitted by Tom Buras)*

On the Brandeis Runway

Dorothy Griswold models at a Brandeis fashion show held February 12-17, 1951. Brandeis seamstresses sewed fashions from McCall's and Simplicity patterns, and other Brandeis employees modeled the clothing. Dorothy worked in the linen department at Brandeis from 1947-51.

(Submitted by Patti Ybarra, daughter of Dorothy)

Brandeis Boogie-Woogie

Eddie Haddad and his Orchestra held dances every Saturday night on the 10th floor of the Brandeis Store in 1951. The parties were attended mostly by high school students, including Lois Shattuck, who went every week.
(Submitted by Lois Shattuck)

Kelly Girls

Kelly's Bowling Alley, 16th and Harney Streets, was home territory for the Northern Natural Gas Co. bowling league in 1951. In foreground, from left are Betty Ern Popek, Betha Mae Cissna, Glorice Hill Hansen and Mary Satory Macrander.
(Submitted by Betty Popek)

Preparing for the 1952 Flood

OPPD workers sandbag the northside of a power plant water tower in advance of a major flood in April 1952. Despite homes being underwater, OPPD kept power flowing. During the flood, many OPPD workers were on duty around the clock and found they drank about 10,000 cups of coffee.

(Submitted by Omaha Public Power District)

Flood Relief

Gerry Clark Karasek (back left in white blouse) at work in the Omaha District Office, Army Corps of Engineers at 1709 Jackson St. during the April 1952 Missouri River flood. She met her future husband, Leonard, at the corps, and they married in 1955. *(Submitted by Leonard Karasek)*

Mariachi Men

The Los Hermanos Barrientos band at George's Bar, 27th and Q Streets, in 1952. Left to right: Vidal Barrientos, Juan Barrientos, Gilbert Buso and Panfilo Barrientos. The band also played at home parties in south Omaha. *(Submitted by Dolores Barrientos Hernandez, daughter of Vidal Barrientos)*

Service with a Smile

Carol Piper Davey (left) and Claudette Pape get ready for the lunch crowd at Sprague's Benson Pharmacy, 6103 Maple St., during the summer of 1953. In the early '60s, the cafe went out of business to make room for the expanding pharmacy. The building is now the location of Jane's Benson Health Market and Deli. *(Submitted by Carol Davey)*

Live With Preston Love

The grand opening of the Offbeat Club, 24th and Lake Streets, in 1953 featured (photo at left) the Preston Love Band, including (beginning at second from left) Phylis Love Abrahms, Eddie Eugene, Mrs. Ralph Alexander, Ralph Alexander, club owner Ed Louis and Betty and Preston Love. In 1960 (photo above), the band performed for the Midwest Athletic Club at the Music Box, 19th Street and Capitol Avenue. From left, Rosetta Steele, Donnie Kelly, Noles Patterson, Preston Love, Kenny McDougald, Harry Vann, Calvin Keyes and Bob Frogge. *(Submitted by Preston Love)*

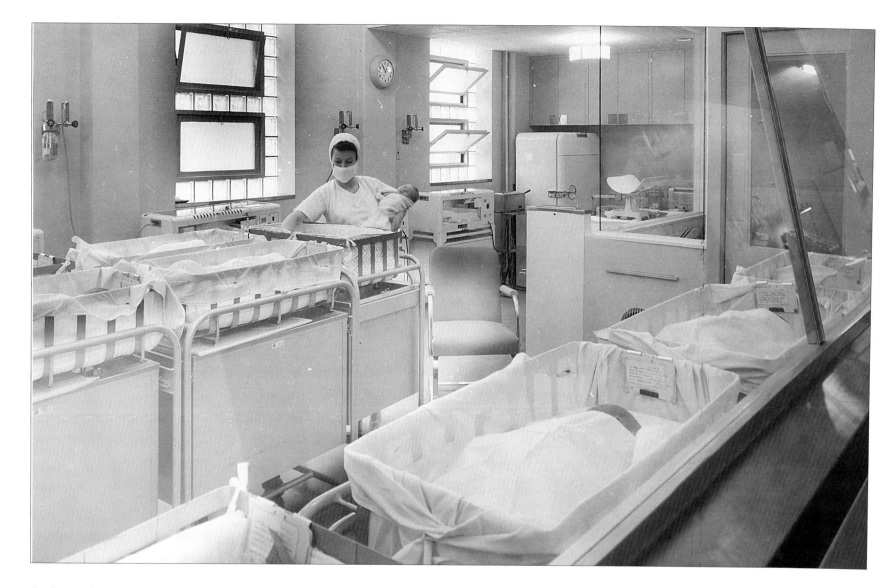

Infant Care at University

Infants undergo check-ups in this 1953 scene at University Hospital, near 42nd Street and Dewey Avenue.

(Submitted by Nebraska Health System)

Riding Into the History Books

From left, Henry Hamann, William Kratville, Richard Orr, Ray Lowry, an unidentified motorman, Loren Hill and John Brunner gather as the last streetcar built in Omaha, No. 1040, leaves 42nd Street and Grand Avenue on March 28, 1953. The city's last streetcar ran March 5, 1955.

(Submitted by Richard Orr, author of a history of Omaha's streetcars)

ABC's on TV

The University of Nebraska at Omaha education department put on kids' television programs at WOW-TV in 1954. Ray Hofmann Jr. (second row, foreground) participates in one of the shows. *(Submitted by Mary Lou Brunson, mother of Ray Hofmann Jr.)*

"Typical Housewife"

The "Typical Housewife" show aired in the fall of 1954 on KMTV. Here, Cecilia McNamara (right) makes a guest appearance in October of that year. *(Submitted by Carolyn McNamara, Cecilia's daughter)*

Fast Pitch Champs

After a 36-12 season, the Phillips Basket Co. Omaha Class A fast pitch softball team went on in 1954 to win the first regional fast pitch tournament, held at the new Boyd Field, 16th and Boyd Streets. Omaha won two of three games against the Hamm's Beer team and was awarded the Greater Omaha and Metropolitan Omaha Championship.

(Submitted by Bud Wilson, a team member)

B-ROW - W. PHILLIPS, W. BASS, A. PETERSON, D. NOVACEK, L. NELSON, W. BORGESON, H. CONNER   F. ROW - R. PHILLIPS, B. WILSON, B. MACKIE, P. TUTTLE, E. REHN, K. KELLEY

PHILLIPS   1954   BASKET
GREATER OMAHA ᴀɴᴅ METROPOLITAN OMAHA CHAMPIONS

Undefeated

The Phil-lettes were champions of the Bon-Femme Class A women's fast pitch softball league in 1954 with an overall record of 16-0. The team won the metro Class A championship, qualifying it for the regional tournament at Boyd Field, 16th and Boyd Streets. The Phil-lettes finished 1-2 in the tournament, losing to the eventual champion. Back row, from left: Coach Don Payne, Angie DeCarlo, Vicki Swiercezek, Doris Hoffman, Joyce Johnson, Midge Moore and Muriel Murphy. Front row, from left: Donna Sletten, Vivian Hodgson, Phyllis Churchill, Joanne Phillips and Joan McMillan.

(Submitted by Bob Phillips, son of team sponsor Phillips Basket Co.)

Curbside Banking

Patt Finn pulls up to the curb to make a deposit at U.S. National Bank (The firm is now part of Wells Fargo Bank). Guard Carl Lindbaugh will drop Finn's money into a deposit box on the sidewalk. The practice, known as curbside banking, was common for many people who banked in the 1950s.

(Submitted by Wells Fargo Bank)

Coronation at St. Ann's

May Crowning at St. Ann Catholic Church, 24th and Poppleton Streets, in 1954. All eighth grade girls were involved along with their attendants. Two attendants were selected to carry Mary's crown and the Queen of May Crowning's crown. To the right of Father Louis Cimino, holding Mary's crown is Mary Lowery.

(Submitted by Mary Lowery Brown)

Clarkson's First Baby

Mary Ellen Detlef was the first baby born at the new Clarkson Hospital, 42nd Street and Dewey Avenue, in 1955.
(Submitted by Nebraska Health System)

The Mimic Macs

The Mimic Macs were popular nightclub and television entertainers from 1949 to 1955. From left, Bob Burt, Hal Perrin and Bob Horton. The men played four shows a night at Charlie's Blue Room, 40th and Leavenworth Streets, along with Angelo's supper club, 1012 S. 10th St., and the Birchwood Club at 27th Street and Redick Avenue. They also performed thoughout the Midwest.
(Submitted by Hal and Helen Perrin)

En Route to Stardom

Bob Boozer, left, graduated in 1955 from Technical High School, where he was a basketball standout under Coach Cornelius Mosser. Boozer went on to become an All-American player at Kansas State University and was a member of the United States' 1960 Rome Olympic basketball team that won a gold metal. After playing professional basketball for the Cincinnati Royals, New York Knicks, Chicago Bulls and the 1977 Championship Milwaukee Bucks, he entered business in Omaha, working in community relations for the telephone company.

(Submitted by Rose Baker)

Up Their Alley

The Women's International Bowling Club hosted its 38th annual championship competition in 1955. Joy Meenths (middle) attends the event with her team partners. *(Submitted by Dorothy Eddy Sciford, Joy's daughter-in-law)*

Dry Cleaning

Ed Elder takes a dry dip in front of the alumni office at Creighton University in 1955. The inside of the building was being remodeled. Ed worked in the maintenance department at Creighton for 40 years. *(Submitted by Shari Elder, Ed's daughter)*

Young Recruits

Outside their home at 27th Street and Ames Avenue in 1957, Ron Wilson (standing) and his brothers Randy (foreground, in cap) and Roger pretend they are in the Army. Occasionally, the boys slept in the tent overnight.

(Submitted by Bud Wilson)

Dapper Dozen

Mr. and Mrs. Julius Yeshnowski and ten of their 12 children form their own Easter Parade near their home at 2226 Hanscom Blvd. in 1958. From left: Mr. Yeshnowski, Richard, Barbara, Mary Jane, Margaret, Dorothy, Virginia, James, Jackie, Rose, Mrs. Yeshnowski and Theresa head to church on Good Friday. *(Submitted by Mary Yeshnowski)*

Conning for Coins

Charles F. Feder was a volunteer for the March of Dimes. To lure donations, Feder would pose as a bum. Here, he is pictured at the Classic Bar, 24th and N Streets, after work in January 1956.
(Submitted by Charles J. Feder, his son)

Crazy for the "King"

An Elvis Presley concert excites a teen-age audience at the Civic Auditorium in 1956. Omaha Police Lt. Magnus Christensen (far left) was in charge of security at the concert. Christensen served 30 years as a police officer and said the concert was his "wildest time on the force."
(Submitted by Richard Christensen, son of Marcus)

Serving Swift for 31 Years

In 1957, Paul Vojchehoske (left, front) is presented a retirement award after 31 years of service to Swift Packing Co., 27th and Q Streets. He and his wife, Pauline (right of Paul), both worked for the company. Paul worked in sweet pickles, and Pauline worked with sausages. *(Submitted by Marsha Polak, granddaughter of Paul and Pauline)*

Cousins on Parade

The annual Papillion Days Parade drew many families from the Papillion area. These kids marched in the July 1955 parade. They called themselves the "Seven Buzzin' Cousins." All are grandchildren of Frank Lorence and Christine Velehradsky Lorence. From left: Doug Lorence, Francine Holubar, Rick Schram, Chris Holubar, Gary Lorence, Don Lorence and Alice Schram. *(Submitted by Chris Holubar Walsh)*

Dressed to Orders

These servicemen, pictured in 1958, worked for the National Cash Register Co. They were required to follow a dress code and drive company Chevrolets. In 1962, this office at 1511 Howard St. was closed. From left: H.J. Lokke, J.A. Wilmes, M.H. Sorum, D.D. Dohse, R.A. Ronneau and C.B. Lloyd.

(Submitted by Henry J. Lokke)

Bluejay Spirit

Creighton University's cheerleaders in 1957.
Joan Calandra next to the mascot.
(Submitted by Joan Calandra Swan)

Carrying on a Family Tradition

From left, Leo J. Hughes and his sons, Jack, Pat, James, Bill, Eddie and Dennis outside their home at 308 N. 37th St. in 1957. Jack, Patrick and James all had evening World-Herald newspaper routes. The boys woke as early as 5 a.m. to deliver the Sunday paper. Jack, Pat and James used the extra money to buy clothes. Their father, Leo, was also a carrier.
(Submitted by Kathleen Hughes, daughter of Leo)

Voices of All Saints

The choir at All Saints Catholic Church, 27th Street and Dewey Avenue, during Christmas 1957.
(Submitted by Catherine Lynn)

A Woodmen History Lesson

Charlie McCarthy and Edgar Bergen meet a bust of Woodmen of the World Life Insurance Society founder Joseph Cullen Root in the Woodmen Home Office museum in 1959. During their visit, Charlie claimed to be a nephew of the wooden stump that was featured in the Woodmen logo.
(Submitted by Woodmen of the World)

Dames and Dudes

The 1959-1960 Dames and Dudes square dance club. In the middle row, on the far left, are Marie and Joseph Trobaugh. The group danced at Sokol Hall during the 1960s. Occasionally, Joseph would call the dances.

(Submitted by Marie Trobaugh)

In Time for Christmas

James Tesarek and his sister, Elsie, assemble a
chair at their mother's home at 18th and
Josephine Streets in December 1959. They
bought the chair for their mother for
Christmas that year so she would be
comfortable at her Singer sewing machine.
(Submitted by Susan Tesarek Bruce, daughter of James)

A Printer at His Trade

Albert E. Grote works with an original Heidelberg Press at the
Ralph Printing Co., 19th Street and St. Mary's Avenue, in 1959.
(Submitted by Herbert Grote, son of Albert Grote)

40 Years on the Scales

Lonnie Rice ran scales for the cattle at the Livestock Exchange Building for 40 years, retiring in 1965.
(Submitted by Rice's grandson Greg Mladovich, and his wife, Mary)

A Four-Generation Business

Bob Pettit carries a rug outside Acme Rug and Carpet Cleaners at 1336 Park Ave. Started in 1927 by Bob's father, Joe, the business has supported four generations of the Pettit family. At one time, all four generations were active in the firm. Acme Rug Cleaners is now operated by Joe's grandson, Roger, and Joe's great-grandson, Matt.
(Submitted by Acme Rug Cleaners)

With JFK in 1960

Women from Duchesne College meet John F. Kennedy at the Fontenelle Hotel in 1960. Kennedy visited Omaha during his presidential campaign. Second from the right is Duchesne student Toni Donohue.

(Submitted by Toni Donohue Fangman)

Macaroni Makers

A 1961 gathering of workers at Skinner Macaroni, 6848 F St. Anne Lowery (front row, second from right) worked at Skinner on and off for about 20 years.
(Submitted by Kitty Schamber, Mary Brown and Kelly Dalhoff, daughters of Anne Lowery)

Peony Park Ballroom

The inside of the Peony Park ballroom, 78th and Cass Streets, in 1970. Joe Malec opened Peony Park in 1917. The ballroom was built six years later. The ballroom was the site for banquets, dances, wakes, roasts, weddings and celebrations and events of all varieties. It seated 1,600 people and served more than 100,000 meals a year. Peony Park was demolished in 1996.
(Submitted by Louie Marcuzzo)

Where "Wild Kingdom" Began

Mutual of Omaha sponsored the television show "Wild Kingdom" from 1963 to 1986. The show, which aired on Sunday evenings, won four Emmy awards and numerous other honors and helped put Omaha on the map. The host was zoologist Marlin Perkins. As head of Chicago's Lincoln Park Zoo, Perkins already had been on television as host of "Zoo Parade" from 1950 until 1957. In this 1978 photo, Perkins, left, is pictured with Mutual Chairman and CEO V. J. Skutt, on the 11th floor of Mutual's headquarters.

(Submitted by Mutual of Omaha)

Setting the Standard

When this picture of Anderson Standard gas station, 30th and Dodge Streets, was taken in 1962, gas was 25 cents per gallon. The station was built in the '30s and torn down during the spring of 2000. The owner, Ray Anderson, now manages stations in west Omaha. *(Submitted by the Ray Anderson family)*

Home Delivery by Harley

Ronnie M. Frizzell attached a sidecar to this Harley Davidson motorcycle while working for a home delivery service. The delivery service, owned by Dean Hummer and located at 1309 N. Saddle Creek Road, made 35 to 40 deliveries per day. This photo was taken in 1961. *(Submitted by Ronnie M. Frizzell)*

Star Who Became a Coach

In the late 1950s and early 1960s, Deanna Grindle played softball and basketball for the Omaha Wrights athletic teams. She was a first team All-American in 1963 in the AAU and was also the national free-throw champion for two years. She was inducted into the Iowa Girls Hall of Fame and went on to coach the Omaha University's women's basketball team.
(*Submitted by Robert I. "Diz" Newton, former coach of Omaha Wrights athletic teams*)

To Baltimore - and Back

In October 1962, the Vandenbergs, a family of 13, boarded a plane that would take them from their hometown of Omaha to a new home in Baltimore, Md., where George Vandenberg had accepted a job. The family included: Michael, Theresa, Jim, Diane, Christine, Steve, Mary, Jeff, Ann, Monica, Matthew and George and Catherine Vandenberg. The family moved back to Omaha in June 1968.
(*Submitted by Ann Vandenberg Wilwerding*)

The Beauties of Mutual

Pictured are the eight finalists for "Ms. Credit Union" in 1962. Front row (left to right); Maureen Stevens, Sue Swanson, Janice Schimonitz, and Nadine Graves. Back row (left to right): Lila Osbahr, Pat O'Day, Rosalie Blank and Connie Coenen. The candidates were nominated by people throughout Mutual of Omaha. Finalists were judged on poise, popularity and professionalism and how they handled themselves in an interview. *(Submitted by Nadine Graves)*

A Wonderful, Wonderful Welcome

Lawrence Welk is welcomed to Omaha in 1965 by Louis Sevek Jr. and Joyce Koutecky, queen of the Sokol Omaha Czech Brass Band. In 1965 Welk and his orchestra performed at the Civic Auditorium. Welk got his start playing in orchestras in the Midlands.
(Submitted by Mary Brau, niece of Louis Sevek)

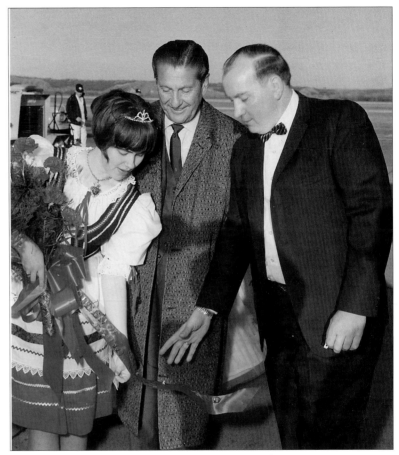

Mustang Power

The Mustangs Football Club owners at Rosenblatt Stadium in 1965. From left, Mike Dugan, Charlie Mancuso, Bob Adwers, Bill Quinlan and Bernie Berigan.
(Submitted by Bob Adwers)

Full-Service and Then Some

These two brothers, Max "Mick" (left) and Milton Moskowitz, owned and operated the Cherry Garden Garage, 3701 Leavenworth St., from 1920 to 1966. It was named for the cherry orchards that once occupied the area. The garage was open 24 hours and offered customers chauffeur service and storage and repair. Another added benefit was the option to drop off a car in the evening and have it serviced for pickup in the morning. *(Submitted by Lois Wine, daughter of Max, niece of Milton)*

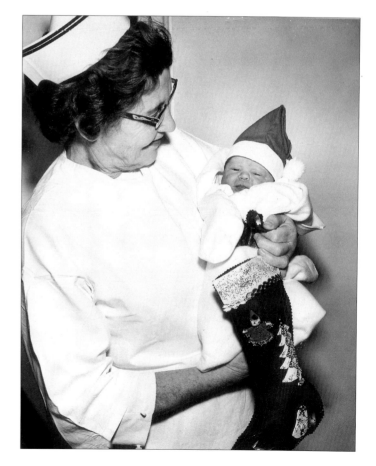

Born on Christmas Day

Gina Ann Verschelde was born on Dec. 25, 1965, at St. Joseph Hospital. Chief Nurse Florence Hanrahan dressed the newborn in an appropriate outfit for her date with a photographer. Nurse Hanrahan also filled Gina's Christmas stocking with plenty of lotions and baby formula. *(Submitted by Kathleen Hoffman, mother of Gina Ann Verschelde Kilzer)*

A Kennedy at Creighton

Sen. Robert Kennedy, D-N.Y., visited Creighton University in May 1968 during the presidential primary campaign. He spoke largely about the Vietnam War. Kennedy wore a tie bar in the image of PT-109, the Navy boat commanded by his brother, the late John F. Kennedy, during World War II. While in Omaha, Sen. Kennedy gave the tie bar to William E. Ramsey who had remarked about his admiration for John Kennedy. Sen. Kennedy won the Democratic primary in Nebraska, defeating Sen. Eugene McCarthy of Minnesota. Less than a month later, he was assassinated in Los Angeles. *(Submitted by William E. Ramsey)*

Mom Always Liked Omaha Best

The Smothers Brothers arrive at the Eppley Airfield to perform at the Nebraska Centennial Ball at Peony Park, March 1967. *(Submitted by Louie Marcuzzo)*

Members of the Omaha Chapter of the Black Panthers in 1969
From left: Robert Cecil, Bobby Griffo, Frank Peak (with eyes closed), Gary House (with glasses) and William Peak.

Homecoming Night Royalty

At the Omaha Central High School homecoming dance on Oct. 7, 1978, candidates for king and queen gathered in the lobby of the Livestock Exchange Building, where the dance was held. The candidates were: First row, from left, Kathy Bohi, Susie Mains, Teri Mancuso, Jackie Washington, Ann Bienhoff and Peggy Zerse. Second row, from left, David Felici, Mark Rigatuso, Grady Hansen, Nate Butler, Tony Jansa and Robert Schuerman. Later that evening, David Felici and Jackie Washington were crowned king and queen.
(Submitted by Howard Marcus)

Bob Hope Comes To Town

Bob Hope performs at the Civic Auditorium in late 1960s.
(Submitted by William E. Ramsey)

The Horse Needed Cash

In the 1970s, cowboy entertainer Monty Montana rode into the lobby of the Omaha National Bank (now US Bank) at 17th and Farnam Streets. The horse wore rubber shoes. Montana was in Omaha for a promotion.

(Submitted by William E. Ramsey)

Teammates for Life

In 1971, Frank Delfano played second base for the University of Southern California, which won the national championship that year in the College World Series. Throughout the series, a young Joe Beal sat in the dugout directly behind the USC players. He developed a friendship with Frank, and the two remained in close contact thereafter.

(Submitted by Joe Beal)

Honoring One of Their Own

A party in 1973 at the Omaha Press Club, 16th and Dodge Streets, honors photographer John Savage (second from left). John retired from the The World-Herald in 1970 after more than 40 years. He served as a state senator in the late 1970s. Also in retirement he helped manage the Press Club. From left, Bill Ramsey, Marie Savage and Howard Silber join John.

(Submitted by William E. Ramsey)

167

Nuclear Power Arrives
The first fuel is loaded into the reactor at OPPD's Fort Calhoun Nuclear Station in 1973.
(Submitted by Omaha Public Power District)

Summer Haven
Peony Park was a regular getaway for teen-agers Robin Spackman (left) and Cindy Siglin, shown with a park employee in 1973. The girls got to the amusement park as often as they could for swimming and the rides.
(Submitted by Cindy Siglin Davis)

The Tornado of '75

Looking west from the Ak-Sar-Ben track during the tornado of May 6, 1975. The track photographer, Bob Dunn, took the picture.

(Submitted by Robert L. "Diz" Newton)

Dealing with the Devastation

A family tries to cope with the aftermath of the May 6, 1975, tornado. With winds of more than 200 mph, the tornado ripped a nine-mile path of destruction from Ralston to Benson, killing three people and injuring hundreds more. It also severely damaged and destroyed 572 homes, two schools and 55 businesses, at a cost of $300 million to $500 million.

(Submitted by the Omaha World-Herald archives)

War and Remembrance

The Korean-Vietnam Peace Memorial was dedicated on Memorial Day, May 30, 1976, at Memorial Park. The monument was dedicated as a tribute to the men and women who served in the Korean War and the Vietnam War.

(Submitted by William E. Ramsey)

Boys Town

Mother Teresa of Calcutta received the Father Flanagan Award for Service to Youth at the Hilton Hotel (now Doubletree) in 1976. She was honored for her work with the poor and dying in India. It was the second time the award had been extended. Mrs. Spencer Tracy, widow of the star of the film, "Boys Town," was the first honoree in 1975. In this photo, Boys Town Mayor Clarence Walker, presents Mother Teresa with a certificate naming her an honorary citizen of Omaha. *(Submitted by William E. Ramsey)*